The Deception of Theistic Evolution

D1825490

Mark Allfree
Matthew Davies

BIBLE STUDY PUBLICATIONS
"Woodlyn", The Park, Mansfield, Nottinghamshire NG18 2AT, UK

First published 2017

© Bible Study Publications 2017

ISBN: 978-1-326-83151-6

Bible Study Publications
"Woodlyn" • The Park • Mansfield • NG18 2AT • UK

Illustrations:

Cover:
https://upload.wikimedia.org/wikipedia/commons/1/14/
Human_evolution_scheme.png

Contents

Preface

"Beloved, when I gave all diligence to write unto you of the common salvation, it was needful for me to write unto you, and exhort you that ye should earnestly contend for the faith which was once delivered unto the saints" (Jude v 3)

This book is essentially a reproduction of a series of articles that were first published electronically on various Christadelphian Facebook discussion forums during 2015 and 2016. There have been some edits to aid continuity, and some additional information has been included to reflect feedback that was received, both positive and negative, from various quarters. Two chapters have also been added on the subject of demons, adapted from John Allfree's booklet, "Demon Possession"[1], to address the assertion that is commonly put forward that other parts of the Bible, outside of the book of Genesis, are unscientific, and are based upon the mistaken beliefs of ancient near eastern civilizations.

The articles were initially produced in an attempt to raise a voice of protest against the growing acceptance of the false notion of theistic evolution within the Christadelphian community. Having examined the matter carefully, we remain firmly of the opinion that theistic evolution is not compatible with the first principles of scripture truth. It is not consistent with the teaching of the scriptures regarding the nature and mortality of man, the entry of sin and death into the world, the atonement and the inspiration of holy scripture, and for these reasons it ought to be vigorously opposed.

---

[1] *"Demon Possession"*, John Allfree, Bible Study Publications, 2001.

It is sad to say that there appears to be a distinct lack of perception within the Christadelphian community that theistic evolution does indeed represent an attack on the fundamentals of the faith, and is not consistent with "the things concerning the kingdom of God, and the name of Jesus Christ"[2]. Our concern is particularly for the younger members of our community, who will inevitably at some point come into contact with the teachings of theistic evolutionists, and who may be swayed by the perceived plausibility of the arguments, without appreciating that they do in fact undermine a number of basic first principle doctrines.

We believe it is the responsibility of all within the brotherhood to be on our guard against such things, and to equip ourselves as best we can with sound Biblical arguments, in order to be able to provide wise counsel to those who are troubled with this perversion of the truth. It is our hope and prayer that this book may assist in this regard.

Mark Allfree
Matthew Davies
Nottingham Forest Road Christadelphian Ecclesia
March 2017

---

[2] Acts 8:12

1. Introduction

"Prove all things; hold fast that which is good" (1 Thessalonians 5:21)

About this book
This book is not an exposition of the early chapters of the book of Genesis - it is not intended to be. There are plenty of other resources available to the Bible student that seek to provide an exposition of the creation account[1]. Neither is it a treatise on science[2]. The objective of this book is to *address from scripture*, by means of a number of carefully selected topics, some of the arguments commonly put forward by the proponents of theistic evolution.

What is theistic evolution?
Theistic evolution - sometimes called "evolutionary creationism" - is a viewpoint that seeks to reconcile the early chapters of Genesis with a modern scientific worldview about biological evolution. Supporters of theistic evolution accept without reservation that scientific discovery has proven

---

[1] The Book of Genesis: The Christadelphian Expositor; H P Mansfield, Logos Publications
Genesis 1-4; H A Whittaker, Biblia Books
Studies in the Truth of Creation; Nigel Bernard, www.lulu.com/spotlight/quayexposition
Genesis 1:1 re-examined, Kel Hammond, www.christadelphianvault.net

[2] For this see "The Bible, Science, Evolution and Creation", Kel Hammond, www.christadelphianvault.net

evolution to be true, and beyond question[3]. They believe that "evolution is real, but it was set in motion by God"[4], and that "evolution occurred as biologists describe it, but under the direction of God"[5]. Theistic evolutionists attempt to reconcile this with the Bible by seeking to demonstrate that Genesis 1 & 2 are not a historical account of how God created the heavens and the earth. They reject the clear teaching of scripture that God created heaven and earth in six literal days, and seek to explain away the early chapters of Genesis by various means.

Varying beliefs of theistic evolutionists

Theistic evolutionists do not all believe the same thing. For example, they have varying opinions regarding the historical reality of Adam. Some claim that Adam is just a metaphorical figure, even a myth; others that he was a real person. Some believe that Adam was the first of a race of beings that came into existence by process of evolution, to whom God chose to reveal Himself. Others believe that whilst humankind came into existence by evolutionary means, Adam was a separate, special creation by God. Those theistic evolutionists who believe that Adam was a special creation nevertheless maintain that Adam's offspring intermarried with a race of humans that did not descend from Adam, but had arisen by an evolutionary process over millions of years, prior to Adam's creation.

---

[3] The authors of this book are aware that the term "evolution" has changed over time and that modern definitions of it have become wide and varied. We have no problem accepting what is currently called "micro-evolution", that is, changes in gene expression within populations of a *particular species*, leading to beneficial adaptation to a particular environment. This has been demonstrated beyond doubt (e.g. in dog or horse breeding, the development of antibiotic resistance in bacteria etc.). We do, however, firmly reject the notion of "macro-evolution" - the supposition that life could have originated in the first place without Divine intelligence, or that one species could evolve into a *completely new species* by incremental genetic changes over long periods of time. Macro-evolution has never been scientifically demonstrated, and it runs contrary to the revealed truth of scripture.

[4] Francis Collins: "Building bridges". Nature 442 (7099): 110. 2006

[5] Stipe, Claude E., "Scientific Creationism and Evangelical Christianity", American Anthropologist, New Series, Vol. 87, No. 1 (Mar., 1985), p. 149, Wiley on behalf of the American Anthropological Association

As far as the book of Genesis is concerned, there are again differing points of view amongst theistic evolutionists. Some say that Genesis 1 & 2 have no bearing on actual historical events. They are simply teaching stories, based on the beliefs of other ancient near eastern civilizations. Others maintain that in fact nothing at all in *the first eleven chapters of Genesis* should be considered as actual historical fact.

Whilst there are divergent views amongst theistic evolutionists as to how the creation account should be interpreted, all theistic evolutionists agree on one thing - that as far as the creation record is concerned *the Bible does not mean what it says*. When God states that "in six days the LORD made heaven and earth, the sea, and all that in them is, and rested the seventh day"[6], this statement cannot be accepted at face value as a statement of simple fact. In their view, science - by which is meant the beliefs of modern mainstream scientists - is more authoritative than the simple teaching of scripture, and it is scripture that has to accommodate to modern scientific thought, rather than the other way round.

The Bible the only authority

As Christadelphians, we believe that "all scripture is given by inspiration of God, and is profitable for doctrine, for reproof, for correction, for instruction in righteousness"[7]. We reject wholeheartedly the theistic evolutionist's approach to the Bible. We believe that theistic evolution, in its many different forms, is a pernicious teaching, that is capable of making shipwreck of faith. It undermines a number of key first principle doctrines that have been uniquely taught within the Christadelphian community for over 150 years, including the nature of man, how sin and death entered into the world, the supreme authority and inspiration of the word of God, and the atonement.

History of theistic evolution

Theistic evolution is not a new view - it has been developed over many years. It is now taught, in one form or another, in mainstream Protestant

---

[6] Exodus 20:11

[7] 2 Timothy 3:16

christianity[8], and indeed it is the official position of the Catholic church[9]. What is comparatively new is its emergence within the Christadelphian community, and it is being promulgated widely, especially via the medium of social media and internet discussion forums. We believe that if this is not challenged, it will find acceptance, especially within the minds of young people. Our concern is that if this were allowed to continue unchecked it would contribute to the demise of the community as a whole, should the Lord remain away. Sadly, the promotion of theistic evolution within our midst has already led to loss of faith for some[10].

Contend earnestly for the faith

This is why this little book has been written. It is a sincere attempt to sound an alarm, to alert brethren and sisters in Christ to the dangers of the teaching of theistic evolution, and to furnish them with robust scriptural arguments in defence of the Truth. Of course, we accept that Genesis 1 & 2 contains things that are difficult to understand, and we do not claim to have all the answers - far from it. We also accept that there must be a degree of openness of mind amongst us, and a willingness to consider points of view divergent from our own regarding what are admittedly difficult parts of scripture. Nevertheless at the same time we firmly believe that there is such a thing as *the Truth*, characterised by "the things concerning the kingdom of God, and the name of Jesus Christ"[11], and it is our responsibility to defend the Truth against all attempts to undermine and subvert it. The apostle Paul did not mince his words when he wrote, "But though we, or an angel from

---

[8] For example see "Creation and Science", The Episcopal Church

[9] "New knowledge leads to the recognition of the theory of evolution as more than a hypothesis". Message to the pontifical academy of sciences: on evolution, Pope John Paul II, 22nd October 1996
"He created beings and allowed them to develop according to the internal laws that he gave to each one, so that they were able to develop and to arrive and their fullness of being". Francis inaugurates bust of Benedict, emphasizes unity of faith, science, Catholic News Agency, 27th October 2014

[10] "An End of Faith": Rob Hyndman, 29th July 2013.
http://robjhyndman.com/musings/unbeliever/#more-2410

[11] Acts 8:12

heaven, preach any other gospel unto you than that which we have preached unto you, let him be accursed"[12], and this serves to highlight the fact that as custodians of the Truth, it is our duty to "earnestly contend for the faith which was once delivered unto the saints"[13]. Any interpretation of scripture that challenges "those things which are most surely believed among us"[14] must itself be challenged and firmly rejected. Theistic evolution, we believe, is one such false interpretation of scripture, and we have no hesitation in rejecting it for the reasons we outline in this book.

---

[12] Galatians 1:8

[13] Jude v 3

[14] Luke 1:1

2. The Two Books

"All scripture is given by inspiration of God, and is profitable for doctrine, for reproof, for correction, for instruction in righteousness" (2 Timothy 3:15)

Introduction

Before embarking upon a study such as this, it is important to emphasize that our conclusions must be firmly rooted upon *the teaching of scripture alone, and nothing else.* There is no other authority that can form the basis of faith and understanding. The Word of God alone "giveth light; it giveth understanding unto the simple"[1]. As far as saving truth is concerned, the light of understanding can only be found in the Bible. This essential truth is at the heart of the Christadelphian movement. In 1848 the founder of the Christadelphian community, John Thomas, wrote this: "Let us believe nothing that comes from "the pulpit", "the altar", or the press, not demonstrated by the grammatical sense of the scriptures. Let us be contented with nothing less than a "thus it is written", and a "thus saith the Lord"; for He has laid it down in His law, that no one is worthy of belief who does not speak after this rule. "To the law and to the testimony, if they speak not according to this word, it is because there is no light in them" *(Isaiah 8:20)*"[2]

---

[1] Psalm 119:130

[2] J. Thomas, *Elpis Israel,* page 6, 14th edition.

The witness of creation

We make no apology for stressing the importance and absolute authority of the word of God as far as saving truth is concerned. That is not to say that God does not leave Himself without witness in other ways, in addition to His word - of course He does. Evidence of God's creative work can be seen all around us in the wonders of nature; and the vastness of the universe - beyond comprehension by mortal man - gives ample testimony to His existence and His power. Indeed, one of our hymns[3] proclaims this self-evident truth:

> "The spacious firmament on high,
> With all the blue ethereal sky,
> And spangled heavens - a shining frame -
> Their great Original proclaim…
>
> …In reason's ear they all rejoice,
> And utter forth a glorious voice;
> For ever singing, as they shine,
> The hand that made us is Divine"[4]

Observation of the wonders of creation, and the incredible complexity and order in the universe, compels a reasonable person to conclude that there must be an all-powerful and all-wise Creator. At the same time, one is driven to acknowledge the insignificance of man in the grand scheme of things, as was David, when by inspiration he said, "When I consider thy heavens, the work of thy fingers, the moon and the stars, which thou hast ordained; what is man, that thou art mindful of him? and the son of man, that thou visitest him?"[5].

[3] Hymn 128, Christadelphian Hymn Book, 2002

[4] Joseph Addison (1672 - 1719)

[5] Psalm 8:3,4

The two books

Some of our early brethren, recognising the power of the witness of creation, put forward the idea that God has "written" two books[6] - the book of God's *word*, and the book of His *works* - and since God is the Author of both "books", we should expect harmony and consistency between them both. It must nevertheless be emphasized that the Bible clearly teaches that *the Scriptures themselves* are authoritative, and contain the whole testimony of God regarding His purpose. It is only our understanding of God's purpose revealed in the Scriptures that is able to bring us to salvation.

The purpose of this chapter is to illustrate that those today who subscribe to the notion of theistic evolution take the "two books" concept to an unjustifiable extreme. In a bid to elevate the importance of science for the disciple of Jesus Christ, it is argued by some theistic evolutionists that in order to obtain a complete picture of God *and His purpose* it is imperative that we "read" both "books". Thus:

---

[6] For example in an article entitled "The Challenger Answered", Brother Thomas responds to a critic (Mr. L.) of the belief of the mortality of the soul with the following rebuttal: "We fully and cordially admit that a belief in the Bible is necessary before anyone can accept our teaching, or exposition of "the faith once delivered to the saints." No one can confer upon our teaching a higher commendation than this. An intelligent belief of the Bible incapacitates a man from being an honest adherent to the sentiments of all Christendom... Mr. L. "believes the soul immortal, with or without the Bible." We venture to affirm that he can find no testimony in the Scriptures for any such belief; that "without the Bible" all the testimony in "the Book of Nature" (the Bible of unbelief, which unbelievers know as little how to read aright, as they do the prophets and apostles), is to prove the absolute mortality of man. The "Book of Nature" is silent as the grave upon the subject of immortality; and presents us in all the varieties of its living creatures, not one that is exempt from death and corruption. Seeing, then, that neither the Bible nor "the Book of Nature" supplies any testimony to the existence of an "immortal soul" in mortal man, Mr. L. cannot "believe" it; for "no testimony, no faith." Therefore, he can only think there is—certainty he has none. "Creation," he says, "is a failure" if there be no immortal soul in man. We cannot see how it should be so. By "creation," we presume he means, the creation of the human race. The "failure" depends upon the purpose for which the race of man was created. Apart from the Bible, Mr. L., nor any one else, can tell why it was created. The book of Nature does not inform us. From this Bible of the infidel or deist, we can get no response as to the questions— "What are we? And whence came we? What shall be our ultimate existence? What's our present? Are questions answerless, and yet incessant." Answerless, indeed, by any other teaching than the Bible's." *The Christadelphian*, 1884, Volume 21, page 147. It is instructive to note how that, whilst Brother Thomas acknowledges the two books concept, that he only accepts the authority of scripture to give meaning to what is observed in nature.

- "The book of nature is clearly revelatory of God's providential work in Christ, and even non-believers are capable of comprehending its complete order through the proper use of reason and experience (i.e. science properly understood)"[7].
- "The book of scripture is clearly revelatory of God's providential work in Christ, and therefore is true and authoritative in all matters. The problem is that we often misinterpret scripture by imposing our own preconceptions upon it rather than allowing it to speak for itself"[8].
- "The book of creation gives us a picture of God and the world that we may not see if we were to read only the Bible... These two books - the book of creation and the book of scripture - are perhaps best read together, one in each hand"[9].

These writers are not just saying that the wonders of creation testify to the existence of God. In some way God's "providential work in Christ" is revealed through the observation of nature, and God is revealing His purpose to us through creation. Some even go to the extreme of saying that when we observe the handiwork of God in nature, God is actually speaking to us by the Holy Spirit: "By the Holy Spirit, God speaks to us through creation, and science is a tool that helps us to understand what God has to say"[10]. Science is thus no longer viewed as simply the discovery of physical reality - it is viewed as having a theological function: "The scientific enterprise is in many ways *sacred work*, for it is the attempt to understand more fully the handiwork of God, and is in this way not unlike disciplined reading and discerning the Word of God in Holy Scripture"[11].

---

[7] Mark H. Mann, "Augustine of Hippo and Two Books Theology, Part 2", Biologos
http://biologos.org/blogs/archive/augustine-of-hippo-and-two-books-theology-part-2

[8] ibid

[9] Sam Hamilton-Poore, "Reading the "Two Books" of God", Patheos
http://www.patheos.com/Resources/Additional-Resources/Reading-the-Two-Books-of-God

[10] Mark H. Mann, "The Church Fathers and Two Books Theology: Introduction", Biologos.
http://biologos.org/blogs/archive/the-church-fathers-and-two-books-theology-introduction

[11] ibid

The theistic evolutionists emphasize that these two books of God must be in complete harmony, and cannot contradict each other. Any apparent contradiction is down to the inability of the "reader" of the two books to fully understand either one, or the other, or both of them: "God's two books can and should be read together in harmony when we are open to allowing them to speak for themselves on their own terms. Ultimately, they cannot contradict each other because the source of both is the same God and if they seem to be in contradiction it is because we have misread one or both of them, and we need to be willing therefore to allow ourselves to be open to thinking about either one in different ways, trusting that God will ultimately lead us to see the truth of the whole"[12]. Of course, there is an element of truth in this. God is unchanging[13], and it is reasonable that we should expect consistency between His words and His works. But it is assumed, we believe wrongly, that modern science has correctly interpreted the "book" of God's works. The advocates of theistic evolution maintain that science has proven beyond all doubt that evolution is true, and therefore it must be our *understanding of the Bible* that has to be updated, and brought into line with modern scientific "fact", in order to avoid contradiction between the two "books".

How, then, does the theistic evolutionist reconcile the Genesis account with modern evolutionary thought? One method is by maintaining that the Genesis account of creation was never intended to be understood literally. Man's modern understanding of science, which is assumed to be correct, dictates that Genesis 1 and 2 cannot be records of historical fact and so, it is insisted, must be understood in a non-literal way. Herein lies the potential danger of the "two books" idea, when pressed too far. If it is assumed that science has a theological function, just like the Bible does, and scientists have "proven" that evolution is true, then it must be our understanding of the Bible that is at fault, and must therefore change.

---

[12] Mark H. Mann, "Augustine of Hippo and Two Books Theology, Part 2", Biologos
http://biologos.org/blogs/archive/augustine-of-hippo-and-two-books-theology-part-2

[13] See Malachi 3:6, Psalm 33:11, Hebrews 6:17; James 1:17

One writer states: "In Christian belief, God reveals himself in both the written book of the Bible and the created "book" of the natural world. Because of the consistent character of God, these two cannot conflict. Yet at times they seem to say contradictory things to us about the origin and shape of God's creation. What do we do when the results of science disagree with common biblical interpretations? One response is to say that the Bible is right and science is wrong, but this often elevates a particular biblical interpretation to the authority of the Bible itself. Scripture is always given and received within a cultural context. As we attempt to understand the Bible in today's context, Christians sometimes disagree on the meaning of particular passages. Some scriptural teachings, like the accounts of Jesus' death and resurrection, have clear meanings that have been affirmed by the church throughout the centuries and around the world. Other teachings, like the baptism of adults vs. infants, are ambiguous and their interpretation has been debated for centuries... Just as the Bible is always interpreted by fallible humans, so too science is the human interpretation of nature. Thus, its theories are subject to critique and revision... After theories are tested and refined by many scientists all over the world, they give an *ever more reliable* interpretation of physical reality. This is true of many aspects of evolutionary theory, which have been tested and confirmed by numerous scientists in many fields over a long period of time"[14]. Note how that evolutionary theory is once again put forward as being a reliable fact, because it has supposedly been tested and confirmed by numerous scientists, and therefore our interpretation of the Bible has to conform with it. We would, in passing, point out that anyone who claims that the Bible is ambiguous on the matter of adult vs. infant baptism should be viewed with considerable suspicion[15].

It is worth reiterating that nowhere in Scripture is nature ever described as a book of God that must be "read". The Bible teaches that *the Scriptures themselves* are authoritative, and contain the whole testimony of God. It is our

---

[14] "Can science and Scripture be reconciled?", Biologos
http://biologos.org/common-questions/christianity-and-science/scientific-and-scriptural-truth

[15] See M Davies, "Is Infant Baptism Scriptural", The Gospel Truth
http://www.the-gospel-truth.info/is-infant-baptism-scriptural/

understanding of God's purpose revealed in the Scriptures that is able to bring us to salvation, not science. At this point we should emphasize that, whilst our early brethren did sometimes subscribe to the concept of God's two books, *none of them ever entertained the notion of theistic evolution.*

History

The idea of God's two books is not new. In the 17th century Francis Bacon and Galileo Galilei put forward the same idea in order to elevate the status of science in the minds of men and women to that of equal partner with the Bible in the search for truth. In 1605 Francis Bacon published a book entitled *"The Advancement of Learning"*, in which he urged his readers not to "think, or maintain, that a man can search too far, or be too well studied in the book of God's word, or in the book of God's works, divinity or philosophy, but rather let us endeavour an endless progress or proficience in both"[16]. Clearly, although Francis Bacon considered the book of nature to be independent from the book of Scripture, he nevertheless believed it could function somehow as a religious "text". By showing us evidence of the wisdom and power of God, science had a vital theological dimension. On the title page of his book, Bacon depicted knowledge as a ship, passing through the Pillars of Hercules, leaving the waters of ancient knowledge behind for the new ocean of modern knowledge lying beyond it, yet to be fully explored. The two pillars represent science, and philosophy.

It is interesting that Charles Darwin himself quoted this very passage from the writings of Francis Bacon, opposite the title page in his original edition of *"On the Origin of Species"*. Clearly Darwin saw the merit of elevating the status of science in the minds of his original readers, who for the most part still believed in the existence of God.

Galileo Galilei believed that nature was mathematically unambiguous, and it could help us to interpret the book of Scripture, which was, after all,

---

[16] Francis Bacon, "*The Advancement of Learning*", 1605.
http://www.gutenberg.org/ebooks/5500

sometimes verbally obscure.[17] This viewpoint finds resonance with today's theistic evolutionists, who maintain that evolution is a fact confirmed by science, and therefore it has to be the words of scripture that are ambiguous, and must be interpreted in a non-literal way. This point of view is typical of that promoted by theistic evolutionists: "Scientific data can sometimes serve as God's way of warning us when we are standing too close to the scriptural "picture," or at the wrong angle, or with the wrong expectations. The purpose of science is not to verify nor to add to inspired Scripture, but science can help us *eliminate improper ways of reading it.* Likewise, Christians should thoughtfully and appropriately encourage science to rigorously *test its own theories and question its*

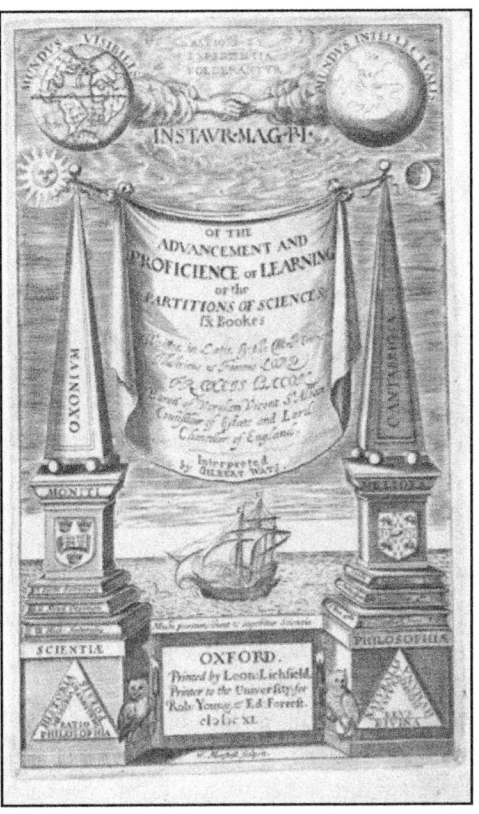

The title page of Francis Bacon's book: *The Advancement of Learning*

---

[17] "With regard to this argument, I think in the first place that it is very pious to say and prudent to affirm that the holy Bible can never speak untruth—whenever its true meaning is understood. But I believe nobody will deny that it is *often very abstruse,* and may say things which are quite different from what its bare words signify. Hence in expounding the Bible if one were always to confine oneself to the unadorned grammatical meaning, one might fall into error. Not only *contradictions and propositions far from true* might thus be made to appear in the Bible, but even grave heresies and follies... It is necessary for the Bible, in order to be accommodated to the understanding of every man, to speak many things which appear to differ from the absolute truth so far as the bare meaning of the words is concerned. But Nature, on the other hand, is inexorable and immutable; she never transgresses the laws imposed upon her, or cares a whit whether her abstruse reasons and methods of operation are understandable to men". Galileo Galilei, *Letter to Madame Christina of Lorraine, Grand Duchess of Tuscany,* 1615. http://inters.org/Galilei-Madame-Christina-Lorraine

own assumptions, especially when science appears to contradict Scripture"[18]. Note first of all how emphasis is given to the idea of God speaking to us through science. Secondly, observe how that once again it is *our interpretation of Scripture* that we are encouraged to bring into line with current accepted science, rather than the other way round. Science - by which is meant the theories of current scientists - is the touchstone against which Scripture must be measured.

Science

It is not true that evolution "has been tested and confirmed by numerous scientists"[19]. There is no direct, observable experiment that can ever be performed that can prove evolutionary theory about the origins of life as fact and that completely different kinds of animals can evolve from common ancestors. Scientists may be able to study mutations in living organisms, observe similarities in morphologies of plants and animals, measure bones and decode DNA, but it is just not possible for them to test postulated evolutionary events in the past. Further, not all scientists accept the theory of evolution as true. There are many eminent scientists today who reject the theory of evolution as scientific fact[20].

Science is changing all the time. What may be considered today to be scientific fact may turn out to be rejected in years to come. It is therefore very difficult to see how any faith can be placed in the shifting sands of current scientific thought. For this reason alone, it would be foolhardy to assume that science has proven the evolutionary origins of life to be true, and therefore that it is necessary for our understanding of Genesis 1 and 2 to accommodate evolutionary theory.

---

[18] Can science and Scripture be reconciled?, Biologos
http://biologos.org/common-questions/christianity-and-science/scientific-and-scriptural-truth

[19] ibid

[20] See: (1) *Darwin Skeptics: A Select List of Science Academics, Scientists, and Scholars Who are Skeptical of Darwinism*, 8/24/2014 Compiled by Jerry Bergman PhD. http://www.rae.org/pdf/darwinskeptics.pdf (2) *Scientists, PhD's and Professors who Question Evolution*, Kel Hammond, www.christadelphianvault.net

A mixture of truth and error

It is perfectly reasonable to expect consistency between God's word and His works. Nevertheless the "two books" concept can be pressed too far, and used to accommodate the theories of fallible scientists, at which point it becomes quite dangerous and potentially subversive of the truth. The irony is that the vast majority of scientists today who believe in evolutionary theory have no time at all for belief in God, and especially for the concept of theistic evolution.

1) **It is TRUE** that the wonder of creation testifies to the existence of a Creator. The complexity of life, the sheer majesty and scale of the universe, and the mathematical precision and order of the cosmos, all cry out for the existence of an omnipotent, all-wise Being who brought things into existence in the first place. Anyone who observes the heavens, and the miracle of life on the earth, ought to be driven to conclude that God exists, and the scriptures give ample testimony to this truth:

- "I will praise thee; for I am fearfully and wonderfully made: marvellous are thy works; and that my soul knoweth right well"[21].
- "The hearing ear, and the seeing eye, the LORD hath made even both of them"[22].
- "By the word of the LORD were the heavens made; and all the host of them by the breath of his mouth"[23].
- "I have made the earth, and created man upon it: I, even my hands, have stretched out the heavens, and all their host have I commanded"[24].
- "When I consider thy heavens, the work of thy fingers, the moon and the stars, which thou hast ordained; What is man, that thou art mindful of him?"[25]

---

[21] Psalm 139:14

[22] Proverbs 20:12

[23] Psalm 33:6

[24] Isaiah 45:12

[25] Psalm 8:3-4

- "Thou art worthy, O Lord, to receive glory and honour and power: for thou hast created all things, and for thy pleasure they are and were created"[26].

But it is NOT TRUE that we *need* science to help us conclude that God exists[27]. There are other, equally compelling reasons, for drawing the conclusion that God must exist, such as:
- The wonder of fulfilled Bible prophecy[28].
- The evidence of archeology which testifies to the truth of the Bible[29].
- The historical accuracy of the Bible, proving its reliability[30].
- The internal harmony and consistent message of the Bible[31].
- The Bible's medical and hygiene laws, ahead of their time[32].

2) It is TRUE that the Bible uses non-literal language of symbol and metaphor to describe God's creative work. For example:

---

[26] Revelation 4:11

[27] It is sometimes suggested that this is the point being made in Romans 1:18-32, but we would suggest that a careful reading and consideration of this passage indicates that the "creation of the kosmos" (v20) which is being described is a reference to the Jewish order and not to the literal creation of Genesis 1.

[28] See: (1) *Wonders of Prophecy: The testimony of fulfilled prediction to the inspiration of the Bible,* John Urquhart, Pickering & Inglis Ltd, 1939. (2) *Evidence of the Truth of the Christian Religion, Derived from the Literal Fulfilment of Prophecy,* Alexander Keith, DD, William Whyte & Co, 1847. (3) The Value of Fulfilled Prophecy, Tony Benson, The Christadelphian Vol 130, April 1993

[29] See: (1) *Evidence for Truth, Vol 2, Archaeology,* Dr E K Victor Pearce, Evidence Programmes, Eastbourne, Sussex, 1993. (2) *Through the British Museum - With the Bible,* Brian Edwards, Clive Anderson, Day One Publications, 2004. (3) *Ten Top Biblical Archaeology Discoveries,* Various authors, Biblical Archaeology Society 2011

[30] See: (1) *Historical Accuracy of the Bible,* The Christadelphian, Volume 10, Page 109 (2) *The Bible and the Critic,* I. Collyer. The Christadelphian, Volume 65, Page 549

[31] See: (1) *Undesigned Scriptural Coincidences,* JJ Blunt, Christadelphian Magazine & Publishing Association Ltd (2) *The Evidences of Revelation,* George Lowe, The Christadelphian, Volume 19, Page 263

[32] See: *The Bible and Medicine,* John Hellawell, Christadelphian Auxiliary Lecturing Society

- Hannah speaks of God setting the world on pillars: "He raiseth up the poor out of the dust, and lifteth up the beggar from the dunghill, to set them among princes, and to make them inherit the throne of glory: for the pillars of the earth are the LORD'S, and he hath set the world upon them"[33].
- God is said to have stretched out the heavens "as a curtain", and like "a tent to dwell in"[34].

But it is NOT TRUE that the meaning of the word of God is verbally obscure, and we need science to help us interpret it properly. This error arises out of a hyper-literal reading of the Scriptures. We have to learn to recognise that God uses symbolic and descriptive language to help us comprehend the greatness and majesty of His works. This does not make the words of Scripture any less true. Every word of God is true:

- "Sanctify them through thy truth; thy word is truth"[35].
- "Study to shew thyself approved unto God, a workman that needeth not to be ashamed, rightly dividing the word of truth"[36].

3) It is TRUE that God created the heavens and the earth by means of His Spirit power:

- "He hath made the earth by his power, he hath established the world by his wisdom, and hath stretched out the heavens by his discretion"[37].
- "In the beginning God created the heaven and the earth. And the earth was without form, and void; and darkness was upon the face of the deep. And the Spirit of God moved upon the face of the waters"[38].

---

[33] 1 Samuel 2:8

[34] Isaiah 40:22

[35] John 17:17

[36] 2 Timothy 2:15

[37] Jeremiah 10:12

[38] Genesis 1:1,2

But it is NOT TRUE that when we observe nature, God is speaking to us by the Holy Spirit. There is no scriptural evidence to support this idea.

4) It is TRUE that nature can teach us wonderful lessons for life, indeed the Bible counsels us to learn from God's creation:

- "Go to the ant, thou sluggard; consider her ways, and be wise: which having no guide, overseer, or ruler, provideth her meat in the summer, and gathereth her food in the harvest"[39]. A warning against slothfulness.
- "Canst thou bind the sweet influences of Pleiades, or loose the bands of Orion? Canst thou bring forth Mazzaroth in his season? or canst thou guide Arcturus with his sons? Knowest thou the ordinances of heaven? canst thou set the dominion thereof in the earth? Canst thou lift up thy voice to the clouds, that abundance of waters may cover thee?"[40]. An exhortation to humility, and a lesson about God's infinite wisdom and power.
- "And why take ye thought for raiment? Consider the lilies of the field, how they grow; they toil not, neither do they spin: and yet I say unto you, that even Solomon in all his glory was not arrayed like one of these. Wherefore, if God so clothe the grass of the field, which to day is, and to morrow is cast into the oven, shall he not much more clothe you, O ye of little faith?"[41]. A lesson to trust in God's gracious provision.
- "When I consider thy heavens, the work of thy fingers, the moon and the stars, which thou hast ordained; what is man, that thou art mindful of him? and the son of man, that thou visitest him?"[42]. A further lesson in humility, and the greatness of God.
- "Now learn a parable of the fig tree; When his branch is yet tender, and putteth forth leaves, ye know that summer is nigh: so likewise ye, when ye

---

[39] Proverbs 6:6-8

[40] Job 38:31-34

[41] Matthew 6:28-30

[42] Psalm 8:3,4

shall see all these things, know that it is near, even at the doors"[43]. A lesson in personal preparedness.

But it is NOT TRUE that we can learn about the *Gospel of salvation* from observation of nature. As we have previously noted, some theistic evolutionists believe that "the book of nature is clearly revelatory of God's providential work in Christ"[44], and this is clearly not the case. The Bible is the *only source* of knowledge concerning God's plan of salvation in Christ, and it is not necessary to be an observer of nature, or to have even a rudimentary understanding of science, to be saved.

The Bible is the only source of saving knowledge

This point is so important that it merits repetition. The Bible clearly teaches that salvation from sin and death is bound up in an individual's faith in the Gospel message, as the apostle Paul declares: "For I am not ashamed of the gospel of Christ: for it is the power of God unto salvation to everyone that believeth"[45]. Nowhere in the Bible do we read that we require an understanding of science to appreciate the wonder of the Gospel. Salvation is not in any way dependent upon knowledge of science. It is true that observation of the wonders of science may increase our faith in the existence of God, but it is not essential *for* faith, and we would do well to remember the words of the apostle Paul: "So then faith cometh by hearing, and hearing *by the word of God*"[46]. We are told that "without faith it is impossible to please him: for he that cometh to God must believe that he is, and that he is a rewarder of them that diligently seek him"[47], and such faith can only be developed by hearing the word of God. These Divine words must become the ultimate authority in regards to what we perceive as truth.

---

[43] Matthew 24:32,33

[44] Mark H. Mann, "Augustine of Hippo and Two Books Theology, Part 2", Biologos
http://biologos.org/blogs/archive/augustine-of-hippo-and-two-books-theology-part-2

[45] Romans 1:16. See also Galatians 3:8, Mark 16:15-16, Acts 8:12

[46] Romans 10:17

[47] Hebrews 11:6

The word of God is a lamp unto our feet, and a light unto our path[48], and the entrance of that word into our hearts and minds "giveth light; it giveth understanding unto the simple"[49]. If that word is not in us, then the verdict of the prophet is very stark and uncompromising: "It is because *there is no light in them*"[50]. It is a sad fact that this is true of the majority of eminent scientists today. They may be very accomplished in their field, but such accomplishment has not led them to accept the existence of a Creator. In spite of their undoubted wisdom in worldly things, as far as God is concerned there is no light in them. They are "alienated from the life of God through the ignorance that is in them, because of the blindness of their heart"[51]. As far as the scriptures are concerned, they are fools, for "the fool hath said in his heart, There is no God"[52].

The word of God is the means whereby God is able to shine in our hearts, "to give the light of the knowledge of the glory of God in the face of Jesus Christ"[53]. Science cannot do this. Even if the depths of scientific knowledge are plumbed, salvation cannot be gained thereby. But in contrast, "The holy scriptures… *are* able to make thee wise unto salvation through faith which is in Christ Jesus. All scripture is given by inspiration of God, *and is profitable* for doctrine, for reproof, for correction, for instruction in righteousness: *that the man of God may be perfect, throughly furnished unto all good works*"[54].

The truth of this is faithfully encapsulated in the Foundation Clause of the Birmingham Amended Statement of Faith, which is the basis of fellowship for all Christadelphians, thus:

---

[48] Psalm 119:105

[49] Psalm 119:105,130

[50] Isaiah 8:20

[51] Ephesians 4:18

[52] Psalm 14:1

[53] 2 Corinthians 4:6

[54] 2 Timothy 3:15-17

> **THE FOUNDATION** - That the book currently known as the Bible, consisting of the Scriptures of Moses, the prophets, and the apostles, is the only source of knowledge concerning God and His purposes at present extant or available in the earth, and that the same were wholly given by inspiration of God in the writers, and are consequently without error in all parts of them, except such as may be due to errors of transcription or translation (2 Tim 3:16; 1 Cor 2:13; Heb 1:1; 2 Pet 1:21; 1 Cor 14:37; Neh 9:30; John 10:35).

It is therefore to the word of Almighty God that we must turn. It is His word which is the ultimate authority on these matters, not the postulations of the limited and fallible human mind so often exhibited in the ever changing genre of Science. We would therefore do well to view science through the lens of God's revelation rather than view God's revelation through the lens of the theories of science.

3. The firmament of Genesis 1 is not solid

Part 1: The differing opinions of scholars

"And God called the firmament Heaven. And the evening and the morning were the second day" (Genesis 1:8)

Introduction

There is a view that is gaining currency within Christadelphian circles that Genesis chapter 1 is not in fact a true historical account of the origins of the heavens and the earth. It is argued that one of its primary functions is as a polemic[1] against ancient near eastern mythology - an attack on the creation stories of other ancient civilizations. In their stories the universe began as a watery chaos, ruled over by sea monsters. These sea monsters were defeated by the gods, who then argued amongst themselves about the creative plan.

---

[1] "Genesis may well be written as a riposte or polemic against the ANE creation myths common to that time...Genesis makes sense when read against the polytheistic creation myths of the ANE. Genesis shares the common view of the ANE that the earth was flat with a solid firmament and a sun that revolved around the Earth. Where Genesis differs is in its powerful polemic against polytheism. Genesis satirises this idea, and completely subverts it. Whereas the creation myths of the ancients had warring gods making humans as their slaves, Genesis has but one God, creating order from chaos, and making the covenant man in His image. When reading Genesis, we need to avoid reading it as science, but instead read it as theology and polemic. To do otherwise is to miss its powerful message" K Gilmore, *"The ancient near eastern context of Genesis - 5"*, http://berea-portal.com/the-ancient-near-eastern-context-of-genesis-5/

With great effort on their part the universe was brought into being[2]. In stark contrast, the God of the Hebrews, the God of Genesis 1, is the one who created the sea monsters in the first place. God is alone and unopposed in all that He says and does. He speaks and the creative work is done.

It is easy to see how that once it is accepted Genesis 1 is not intended to be understood literally, it is but a short step to conclude that God may have brought His creation into existence by an evolutionary process over millions of years, rather than in six literal days.

Is the firmament in Genesis 1 a solid dome?

A significant foundation stone for the non-literal understanding of Genesis 1 is the assertion that the firmament in Genesis 1 is portrayed by the writer as being solid. The reasoning is that ancient near eastern civilizations believed that the earth was flat, supported by two pillars, and that the firmament was a solid, dome-like structure in which the sun, moon and stars were set. The waters below this firmament represented the seas, and above the solid, dome-like firmament was the ocean of heaven. It is further reasoned that the writer of the book of Genesis, in his description of God's creative work, *assumes that this understanding of the cosmos is correct, indeed he believes it himself.* Since we now know from science that the heavens are not solid, the conclusion is drawn that Genesis 1 does not align itself with modern scientific fact. This therefore gives us liberty to assume that Genesis 1 is not to be understood literally, rather it is a teaching story with, amongst others, a polemical function.

For this reason, a correct understanding of the scripture teaching regarding the firmament has assumed great importance. The approach to Genesis 1 outlined above stands or falls on this issue alone. If it can be demonstrated that this is not the arrangement of the cosmos that is presented by scripture,

---

[2] "In the Babylonian Enuma Elish, one of the most extensive creation accounts that we possess, the world originated this way: first there was a mixing of the primeval fresh and salt waters (called Apsu and Tiamat) to produce the gods, then came a second generation of gods, whose noise disturbed Apsu and Tiamat. When a plan was hatched to destroy the gods, Ea, the god of wisdom, intervened, only to provoke Tiamat to want to attack them further. The other gods, however, turned to the god Marduk, who subsequently defeated Tiamat the sea-monster and with the carcase created the two halves of heaven and earth". *The Biblical creation in its ancient near eastern context*, J Lam. https://biologos.org/uploads/projects/lam_scholarly_essay.pdf

in particularly the book of Genesis, then this case can be dismissed altogether.

The objective of this and the next two chapters is to demonstrate that the firmament (Hebrew רקיע - *raqia*) of Genesis 1 is *not* presented as a solid dome-like structure[3]. This idea can be read into the text if one approaches the Genesis account with this pre-conceived notion, but the text does not demand that understanding of the cosmos. On the contrary, Genesis 1 is an accurate description of the creative work of God in simple terms that anyone, in any age, can understand.

Proponents of the solid dome theory usually make reference to studies by Paul H Seely[4] and Pete Enns[5]. For convenience, we summarise below a number of key assertions that these studies make:
1. The other cosmologies from the ancient world depict some solid structure in the sky. The most rational explanation of the *raqia* in Genesis 1 is that it also reflects this understanding. There is no indication that Genesis is a novel description of the sky.
2. Virtually every description of the *raqia* from antiquity to the Renaissance depicts it as solid. The non-solid interpretation of the *raqia* is a novelty.
3. According to the flood story in Genesis 7:11 and 8:2, the waters above were held back only to be released through the floodgates of the heavens" (literally, "lattice windows").
4. Other Old Testament passages are consistent with the *raqia* being solid (Ezekiel 1:22; Job 37:18; Psalm 148:4).
5. According to Genesis 1:20, the birds fly in front of the *raqia* (in the air), not in the *raqia*.

---

[3] See also: *"Is the firmament of heaven a solid dome?"*, Kel Hammond, www.christadelphianvault.net

[4] "The firmament and the waters above - The meaning of *raqia* in Genesis 1:6-8". Paul H Seely, *The Westminster Theological Journal,* 53 (1991) 227-40

[5] "The firmament of Genesis 1 is solid but that's not the point". Pete Enns, *biologos.org*, Jan 14, 2010

6. The noun *raqia* is derived from a verb that means to beat out or stamp out, as in hammering metal into thin plates. This suggests that the noun form is likewise related to something solid.
7. Speaking of the sky being stretched out like a canopy or tent (Isaiah 40:22), or that it will roll up like a scroll (Isaiah 34:4), are clearly similes which support the view that the *raqia* in Genesis 1 is solid.

Underpinning these articles is the belief that the Genesis account was written by men who adopted the language and understanding of the scientifically naive cultures that existed at the time. As one author on this subject puts it, "We cannot impute to authors knowledge or experience which they could not possibly have had"[6]. It is reasoned that these ideas of ancient civilizations were used and adopted in the Genesis record in order to attack these other gods, and in contrast to show how great the God of the Israelites was. Rather than accepting the divinely revealed explanation of the source of the scriptures - that each word originated from God[7] - advocates of these ideas are telling us that the words of scripture have been limited by the fallible human understanding of the people that wrote the scriptures down in the first place. What is worrying is that these false ideas have begun to be accepted by some Christadelphians. In contrast to the Birmingham Amended Statement of Faith, alternative statements of faith have been posted online. For example, one website that we have come across says this: "Following is a statement of faith representing the Gospel as typically understood by Christadelphians". The first clause reads: "The Bible (as defined by the Protestant canon) is God's inspired Word, *written in the language of its times and reflecting the writers' worldview*"[8]. This is not the Christadelphian

---

[6] "The Three-Story Universe", N F Gier, *God, Reason and the Evangelicals* (University Press of America 1987), Chapter 13. http://www.webpages.uidaho.edu/ngier/gre13.htm

[7] 2 Peter 1:21, 2 Timothy 3:16, Hebrews 1:1, 1 Thessalonians 2:13, Jeremiah 20:9

[8] (1) Berea portal, At statement of faith, http://berea-portal.com/a-statement-of-faith/
(2) Credo, A Personal Statement of Faith, D Burke 2014, https://www.academia.edu/16442218/Credo

position at all[9]. It is this different approach to the authority of scripture which can lead to the accommodation of evolutionary thought.

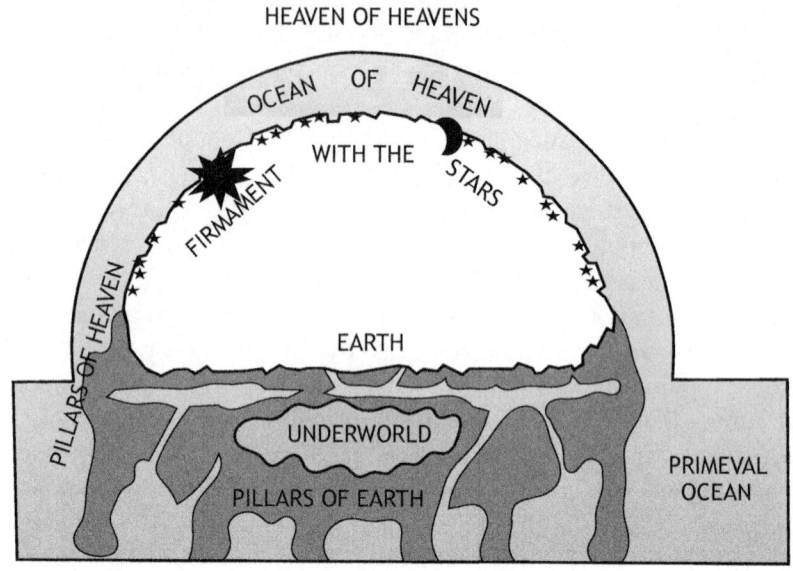

A representative of the beliefs of ancient near east civilizations
regarding the firmament

The beliefs of other civilizations

With regards to the beliefs of other ancient near east civilizations, we do not doubt that some may well have believed that the sky was solid. But it is an assumption to conclude that therefore this is what Genesis 1 is describing. The significant difference between the writings of ancient near eastern civilizations and Genesis 1 is that the latter is the word of the living God, and therefore there is no need to bring Genesis 1 into line with the beliefs of the ancients.

---

[9] See the Christadelphian Statement of Faith (BASF) foundation clause, reproduced on page 21 of this book.

Furthermore, it appears the belief that the sky was solid may not have been as widespread as is being suggested by Seely and Enns. In a study by Randall W Younker and Richard M Davidson[10], we find this statement:

"There have been some who continue to suggest that the ancient Hebrews borrowed cosmological concepts, including the idea of a solid domed heaven, from the Mesopotamians. However, even this idea had to be scuttled when more recent work by Wilfred G Lambert could find no evidence that the Mesopotamians believed in a hard-domed heaven; rather, he traces this idea to Peter Jensen's mistranslation of the term "heavens" in his translation of the Enuma Elish[11]. Lambert's student, Wayne Horowitz, attempted to piece together a Mesopotamian cosmology from a number of ancient documents, but it is quite different from anything found in the Hebrew Bible. Horowitz's study suggests that the Mesopotamians believed in six flat heavens, suspended one above the other by cables. When it came to interpreting the stars and the heavens, the Mesopotamians were more interested in astrology (i.e., what the gods were doing and what it meant for humanity) than they were in cosmology. There is no evidence that the Mesopotamians ever believed in a solid heavenly vault".

The reference that Younker's article makes to Wilfred G Lambert is interesting because Wilfred Lambert was a Christadelphian as well as a historian and archaeologist. He was Emeritus Professor of Assyriology and a worldwide acknowledged authority in languages and civilizations of the Ancient Near East. The whole article is worth reading because it casts considerable doubt upon the dome theory, including the writings of Seely. It gives the lie to the statement of Enns that "biblical scholars understand the *raqia* to be a solid dome-like structure... biblical scholars agree on this understanding of *raqia*". Biblical scholars old and new most certainly do *not* agree.

---

[10] The Myth of the solid heavenly dome: Another look at the Hebrew *raqia*. Randall W Younker & Richard M Davidson, *Andrews University Seminary Studies*, No 1, 125-147, 2011.

[11] "The Cosmology of Sumer and Babylon," Wilfred G Lambert, *Ancient Cosmologies*, ed. C. Blacker and M. Loewe (London: Allen & Unwin, 1975), 42-65.

Here are some quotations from other Biblical scholars who clearly do not agree with Enns' conclusions:

"The most probable meaning of *(raqia)* therefore is *the expanse* or *the expansion*. The LXX rendered it *firmament;* and hence it has been argued that Moses taught the sky to be a hard, metallic vault, in which the sun and stars were fixed; but the most learned modern commentators, including Gesenius, Kalisch &c., believe the true etymology of the word to show that *expanse,* not *firmament,* is the right translation. The teaching, however, of the present passage does not depend on the etymology of the word. If a writer in the present day uses the English word *heaven,* it does not follow, that he supposes the sky to be a vault *heaved* up from the earth. Neither would it follow that the inspired writer had taught, that the portion of atmosphere, intervening between the sea and the clouds, was a solid mass, even if the word used for it had etymologically signified *solidity*"[12].

"We must be careful neither to let our own view of the structure of the universe nor what we might think to have been the view of ancient men control our understanding of the biblical author's description of the "expanse". We must seek what clues there are from the biblical text itself. One such clue is the purpose that the author assigns to the "expanse" in v. 6: it is "to separate water from water". The "expanse" holds water above the land; that much is certain. A second clue is the name given to the *raqia*. In v.8 it is called the "sky". Finally, we should look at the uses of "expanse" within chapter 1. Here the terms refers not only to the place where God put the sun, moon and stars (v.14) but also to that place where the birds fly (v.20: "across the expanse of the sky").... It would be unlikely that the narrative would have in view here a solid partition or vault that separates the earth from the waters above. It appears more likely that the narrative has in view something within the everyday experience of the natural world, in a general way, that place where the birds fly and where

---

[12] Speakers Commentary. *F C Cook,* Commentary on Genesis 1:6. Vol 1 p 33

God placed the lights of heaven (cf. v.14). In English the word "sky" appears to cover the sense well"[13].

"*Raqia* - to stretch, spread out, then beat or tread out, means *expansum*, the spreading out of the air, which surrounds the earth as an atmosphere. According to optical appearance, it is described as a carpet spread out above the earth (Ps. 104:2), a curtain (Isa. 40:22), a transparent work of sapphire (Exod. 24:10), or a molten looking-glass (Job 37:18); but there is nothing in these poetical similes to warrant the idea that the heavens were regarded as a solid mass, such as Greek poets describe. The *raqia* …is called *heaven* in ver. 8, *i.e.* the vault of heaven, which stretches out above the earth. The waters *under* the firmament are the waters upon the globe itself; those *above* are not ethereal waters beyond the limits of the terrestrial atmosphere, but the waters which float in the atmosphere, and are separated by it from those upon the earth, the waters which accumulate in clouds, and then bursting these their bottles, pour down as rain upon the earth. For, according to the Old Testament representation, whenever it rains heavily, the doors or windows of heaven are opened (ch. 7:11,12; Psa. 78:23, cf. 2 Kings 7:2,19; Isa. 24:18). If, therefore, according to this conception, looking from an earthly point of view, the mass of water which flows upon the earth in showers of rain is shut up in heaven (cf. 8:2), it is evident that it must be regarded as above the vault which spans the earth, or, according to the words of Ps. 148: 4, "above the heavens"[14].

"*Raqia* - Identifies God's heavenly expanse. The Mosaic account of creation uses *raqia* interchangeably for the "open expanse of the heavens" in which birds fly (Gen 1:20 NASB), i.e. the atmosphere… and that farther expanse of sky in which God placed "the lights… for signs and for seasons" … In pre-Christian Egypt confusion was introduced into biblical cosmology when the LXX, perhaps under the influence of Alexandrian

---

[13] The Expositor's Bible Commentary. *Frank E Gaebelein*. Commentary on Genesis 1:6. Vol 2 p 29

[14] Commentary on the Old Testament. *C F Keil & F Delitzsch*. Commentary on Genesis 1:6. Vol 1 p 52-54

theories of a "stone vault" of heaven, rendered *raqia* by *stereoma*, suggesting some firm, solid structure. This Greek concept was then reflected by the Latin *firmamentum*, hence KJV "firmament"[15].

"While this English word is derived from the Latin *firmamentum* which signifies firmness or strengthening,...the Hebrew word, *raqia*, has no such meaning, but denoted the "expanse," that which was stretched out. Certainly the sky was not regarded as a hard vault in which the heavenly orbs were fixed.... There is therefore nothing in the language of the original to suggest that the writers were influenced by the imaginative ideas of heathen nations"[16].

Sufficient has been said, and much more could be said, to illustrate that (1) the debate as to the precise meaning of *raqia* is nothing new, and (2) contrary to what Enns says, the scholars do not agree on the etymology of the Hebrew word *raqia*. This, then, leaves us with a dilemma. Which scholars do we choose to believe, and which to reject? The temptation is to choose to accept the opinions of those scholars whose conclusions coincide with our own pre-conceived ideas.

The beliefs of the Mesopotamians regarding the geography of the heavens

It would be as well at this point to summarise some of the beliefs of the ancient Mesopotamians regarding the geography of the heavens. Wayne Horowitz points out that there are two traditions concerning the composition of the heavens[17]. According to one tradition, the heavens are made of water, and in the second they are made of stone.

---

[15] Theological Wordbook of the Old Testament. *R Laird Harris, Gleason L Archer, Bruce K Waltke.* Vol 2 p 862

[16] Expository Dictionary of Old Testament Words, *W E Vine,* Page 67

[17] W Horowitz, *Mesopotamian Cosmic Geography:* The Geography of the Heavens, Ch 11, p 262, 263, Eisenbrauns, Winona Lake, 2011.

1) Water

Babylonian texts explain how the god Marduk stretched out a skin and assigned guards to keep the waters of heaven from draining downwards onto the lower regions of the universe. The phenomenon of rainfall is explained in different ways - some texts connect rainfall with the stars, and in Sumerian texts, rain issues out of cosmic teats which serve as rain ducts in the sky.

2) Stone

The tradition of stone heavens derives from observations that certain heavenly objects were the same colour as minerals. The identification of astronomical bodies with stones, although probably originally based on colour, may have led to a tradition that the heavens themselves are composed of stone. Such a belief might have been confirmed by finding stone meteors that fell from the sky.

Horowitz states that "the extant texts demonstrate that Sumerians and Akkadians understood the universe as consisting of superimposed levels separated by open space. From above to below, the levels were: a region of heaven above the sky where the gods of heaven dwelled, the starry sky, the earth's surface, the subterranean waters of the Apsu, and finally the underworld of the dead"[18]. We should note very carefully that this scheme of the universe bears *no resemblance whatsoever* to the description of the creation of the universe in Genesis 1.

Enuma Elish

The main creation myth to which the Genesis account has been compared by scholars is that of Enūma Elish. Seely, for example[19], quotes this text to establish the Babylonian conception of the sky as a solid roof, and here is the relevant text:

"He [Marduk] split her [Ti'âmat] open like a mussel into two (parts); Half of her he set in place and formed the sky (therewith) as a roof. He

---

18 W Horowitz, Mesopotamian Cosmic Geography, xiii. Eisenbrauns, Winona Lake, 2011.

19 Seely, "The Firmament and the Water Above, Part I", 234

fixed the crossbar (and) posted guards. He commanded them not to let her waters escape".

Wilfred Lambert suggests the following translation of this text:

"He split her into two like a dried fish; one half of her he set up and stretched out as the heavens. He stretched a skin and appointed a watch, with the instruction not to let her waters escape[20]".

A moment's reflection will reveal once again how utterly foreign these ancient concepts of the composition of the universe are to the simple truth revealed in Genesis. We would suggest that it is an insult to the Almighty to even suggest that the inspired Genesis creation account has anything remotely in common with such mythological nonsense.

A Biblical approach

Let us approach the issue another way. All of the so-called scholars are astray from Bible truth on a number of key first principles. None of them understands the Truth of the Gospel in its entirety, as defined by "the things concerning the kingdom of God, and the name of Jesus Christ"[21]. So we may legitimately ask why we should put our trust in any of them, particularly in relation to the exposition of scripture. Why indeed, when there is a much better way, as we have set out in the previous chapters of this book. We should look at scripture as the sole authority and not the writings of men. This is the example we have from scripture. Consider the "noble" Bereans who "searched the scriptures daily" to see whether the things they were being asked to believe by no less a person than the apostle Paul were so[22]. This is not to say that the writings of scholars have no use whatsoever, because after all we rely upon scholars for translating the biblical manuscripts into English in the first place. But as far as the *meaning* of the text is concerned, *the Bible is its own interpreter,* and surely the best way of seeking to understand the

---

[20] W. Lambert, "The Cosmology of Sumer and Babylon", p 55

[21] Acts 8:12

[22] Acts 17:11

meaning of Genesis 1:6-8 is to compare scripture with scripture. As Gaebelein has observed above, "we must seek what clues there are from the biblical text itself".

The next chapter will seek to do just that, and to arrive at an understanding of the firmament in Genesis 1 from the testimony of scripture itself.

4. The firmament of Genesis 1 is not solid
Part 2: What the Bible really teaches

"And God made the firmament, and divided the waters which were under the firmament from the waters which were above the firmament: and it was so" (Genesis 1:7)

Introduction
In the previous chapter it was seen that the belief that Genesis chapter 1 is a real, historical account of the creation of the heavens and the earth is currently being challenged. It is argued by some that the writer of Genesis 1 adopted ideas of ancient near east civilizations, including the belief that the firmament, in which the sun, moon and stars are set, is a solid dome. It is further reasoned that since we now know scientifically that this is not the case, Genesis 1 should not be considered as a true historical account of creation. It it argued it is simply a teaching story, and this approach to Genesis 1 opens the door for the accommodation of evolutionary theory.

In chapter 3 we have shown that scholars are far from united in this understanding of the firmament as a solid dome. This chapter seeks to arrive at a true understanding of the nature of the firmament simply from the testimony of scripture itself. We shall demonstrate that the solid dome theory is not in keeping with the teaching of scripture. Rather, Genesis 1 is a historical account of the creation of the heavens and the earth, and it is absolutely incompatible with the theory of evolution.

God dwells in heaven

We begin from first principles. The scriptures teach us that God Himself dwells in heaven:

- "Be not rash with thy mouth, and let not thine heart be hasty to utter any thing before God: *for God is in heaven*, and thou upon earth: therefore let thy words be few"[1].
- "Hear thou in *heaven thy dwelling place*, and do according to all that the stranger calleth to thee for: that all people of the earth may know thy name, to fear thee, as do thy people Israel; and that they may know that this house, which I have builded, is called by thy name"[2].
- "The LORD is in his holy temple, the LORD's throne is *in heaven:* his eyes behold, his eyelids try, the children of men"[3].
- "He that sitteth *in the heavens* shall laugh: the Lord shall have them in derision"[4].

The scriptures also teach us that God is "from everlasting to everlasting"[5]. He is "immortal, invisible, the only wise God"[6]. This being so, we may reasonably conclude that the heaven in which God dwells *must also have always been*. When, therefore, we read in Genesis 1:1 that *"in the beginning* God created *the heaven* and the earth"*, it follows that the heaven referred to that had a beginning is a different heaven from the heaven in which God dwells.

That this is so is confirmed by the prayer of Solomon at the dedication of the temple, in which he says, "But will God indeed dwell on the earth? behold, the heaven and heaven of heavens *cannot contain thee;* how much less

---

[1] Ecclesiastes 5:2

[2] 1 Kings 8:43; see also vv 30,39,49

[3] Psalm 11:4

[4] Psalm 2:4

[5] Psalm 90:2

[6] 1 Timothy 1:17

this house that I have builded?"[7]. We further conclude from Solomon's words that there is not only a "heaven" which cannot contain God, but also "the heaven of heavens" which cannot contain God. This point is of great significance, and is confirmed by other scriptures:

- "Behold, the *heaven* and the *heaven of heavens* is the LORD's thy God, the earth also, with all that therein is"[8].
- "Thou, even thou, art LORD alone; thou hast made *heaven*, the *heaven of heavens, with all their host,* the earth, and all things that are therein, the seas, and all that is therein, and thou preservest them all; and the host of heaven worshippeth thee"[9].

In Hebrew "the heaven of heavens" is in the construct state and therefore a string of nouns (in this case only two) used to describe one single thing. "The heaven of heavens" is separate from the "heaven". This is a similar style of language to:

- "The holy of holies"[10].
- "Servant of servants"[11].
- "Sabbath of sabbaths"[12].
- "God of gods"[13].
- "Vanity of vanities"[14].
- "Song of songs"[15].

---

[7] 1 Kings 8:27

[8] Deuteronomy 10:14

[9] Nehemiah 9:6

[10] Exodus 26:34

[11] Genesis 9:25

[12] Exodus 31:15

[13] Deuteronomy 10:17

[14] Ecclesiastes 1:2

[15] Song of Solomon 1:1

- "King of kings"[16].

All of these phrases denote the highest order of the particular things being described. Other, lesser, things of the same description are not excluded as being in existence at the same time. For example the phrase "holy of holies" (translated as "Most Holy Place") does not exclude the existence of a "holy place" - in fact it requires it. Therefore "heaven of heavens" is a phrase used to describe the highest and greatest heaven, whilst "heaven" is something lesser. Artaxerxes was a king, but he is described in Ezra 7:12 not merely as a king, but a "king of kings" - the ultimate king. Again, that he is thus described necessitates the existence of other, lesser, kings. Bringing this same logic to "the heaven of heavens" we would expect there to exist a lower realm called simply "heaven".

In the passage quoted from Nehemiah 9:6 we have been provided with the further insight that "the heaven of heavens" is where "all their host" reside - that is, the sun, moon and stars[17].

These scriptures thus clearly demonstrate that, in addition to the heaven in which God dwells, there are two different heavens, styled in Nehemiah "the heaven", and "the heaven of heavens".

The firmament in Genesis

We are now in a position to apply this understanding of the heavens to Genesis 1. Careful reading reveals that the same hierarchy of heavens are present in the text, thus:

1. In **verses 6-8** we read of a specific *"firmament"* which was created to divide the waters above from the waters below. This is called "heaven".
2. In **verses 14-19** we read of the *"firmament of heaven"* (v14 and v17) into which God placed the sun moon and stars. Genesis 1:20 informs us that God created the fowls of the air, to fly "in the face" (NKJV), or in front, of the "firmament of heaven".

---

[16] Ezra 7:12

[17] See Also Deuteronomy 4:19: "thou seest the sun, and the moon, and the stars, even *all the host of heaven*". This proves that Nehemiah's "all their host" denotes the heavenly bodies.

These scriptural distinctions are not appreciated by the advocates of the idea of the solid firmament and it is important to identify them, in order to obtain a clear Biblical view of what is being described and to show that the order of things set out in Genesis is accurate.

The waters above the firmament

Genesis 1:6-8 says, "And God said, Let there be a firmament in the midst of the waters, and let it divide the waters from the waters. And God made the firmament, and divided the waters which were under the firmament from the waters which were above the firmament: and it was so. *And God called the firmament Heaven.* And the evening and the morning were the second day". The work of the second day was thus to create the firmament, called "Heaven". This specific firmament separates the waters below the firmament - the "seas" according to Genesis 1:10 - from the waters above the firmament.

The question is, what do "the waters which were above the firmament" represent? Those who subscribe to the solid dome theory claim that they refer to an ocean of water which the ancient near eastern civilizations believed was situated above the solid dome. But rather that resorting to the writings of ancient near east mythology, let us allow scripture to tell us: "When he prepared *the heavens,* I was there: when he set a compass upon the face of the depth: when he established *the clouds above:* when he strengthened *the fountains of the deep:* when he gave to the sea his decree, that the waters should not pass his commandment: when he appointed the foundations of the earth: then I was by him, as one brought up with him: and I was daily his delight, rejoicing always before him"[18]. These words of the wise man are clearly based upon the Genesis record of creation. The heavens separate "the clouds above" from "the fountains of the deep". We therefore conclude that "the waters which were above the firmament" are "the clouds above".

This is confirmed by the testimony of other scriptures:

---

[18] Proverbs 8:27-30

- "Though he had commanded *the clouds from above*, and opened the doors of heaven"[19]. The clouds are described as "from above" - and using Hebrew parallelism they are equated with "the doors of heaven", from whence the rain comes.
- "For thy mercy is great *above the heavens:* and thy truth reacheth unto *the clouds*"[20]. Again, the parallelism in the verse illustrates that the clouds are "above the heavens".

We can thus conclude that in Genesis 1:8, the "firmament" that God called "heaven" represents the sky, the atmosphere, that intervenes between the clouds and the seas. Clearly this is not solid, and the scripture does not present it to us as if it is solid.

Clouds as windows

Before moving on it might be worth us considering another aspect of the line of reasoning which degrades Genesis to that of a myth with a teaching mechanism. The figurative language used to describe rain is often interpreted by theistic evolutionists as being literal[21]. We are asked to accept that when we read that "the windows of heaven were opened"[22], this represented the view of the ancients regarding the origin of rain - a cosmic ocean above the earth which was held back by a solid dome firmament. Within this solid dome the clouds acted as cosmic portals or windows through which rain could be let in. As we know this is not the case from a scientific perspective, we are then encouraged to dismiss the whole account of Genesis as being literal. Therefore, it is argued, it must all be figurative.

Psalm 78:23 which we quoted earlier is often put forward to support this view: "Though he had commanded the clouds from above, and opened the

---

[19] Psalm 78:23

[20] Psalm 108:4

[21] For example: "The solid firmament that holds back the heavenly waters has "floodgates" or "windows of heaven" that let the water through to flood the earth in Noah's day. (See Gen. 7:11, Gen. 8:2, Isa. 24:18)", Biologos, Brian Godawa, "Mesopotamian Cosmic Geography in the Bible" http://biologos.org/blogs/archive/mesopotamian-cosmic-geography-in-the-bible-part-5

[22] Genesis 7:11. See also Genesis 8:2

doors of heaven…". This is a Hebrew parallelism and is clearly poetic. Because God "commanded the clouds" the "doors of the heaven" were opened. If we adopt a hyper-literal approach to this verse and conclude that the clouds represent portals whereby the waters from cosmic reservoirs above were conveyed to earth, then we must also conclude that God literally spoke to the clouds. On the contrary, this Psalm is simply using a beautiful figure of speech.

Other similar poetic figurative language is found throughout Psalm 78. For example:
- "So a fire was kindled against Jacob"[23].
- "God was their rock"[24].
- "For he remembered that they were but flesh; a wind that passeth away"[25].

We are not intended to conclude from this that God kindled a literal fire amongst His people, or that God is really a rock, or that flesh is really just wind. We have no difficulty in understanding that in all these instances the Psalmist is using symbolic language. God did not literally burn up His people, but He did show His displeasure towards them because they "believed not in God, and trusted not in his salvation"[26]. Flesh is not literally made of wind, but it is transient, and soon passes away. God is not literally a rock, but He is never changing, a firm foundation for our lives. In the same way, the clouds of heaven are not literally portals in the sky. These passages are therefore not descriptions of how the ancients viewed the world around them.

Careful reading of Psalm 78:23,24 reveals that the Psalmist is speaking primarily about the provision of manna in the wilderness, and comparing God's blessing of the manna with the blessing of rain: "Though he had

---

23 Psalm 78:21

24 Psalm 78:35

25 Psalm 78:39

26 Psalm 78:22

commanded the clouds from above, and opened the doors of heaven, *and had rained down manna upon them to eat*, and had given them of the corn of heaven". Just as God opens the doors of heaven and provides rain, so also He rained down manna for His people to eat. Does this mean that the ancients believed in a cosmic reservoir of manna above a solid firmament, that was rained down upon the earth by the opening of portals? Of course not. The Psalmist is using figurative language to describe the blessings that God provided for His people.

This same figure of speech is clearly seen in use in 2 Kings 7:2,19,20: "Then a lord on whose hand the king leaned answered the man of God, and said, Behold, if the LORD would make *windows in heaven*, might this thing be? And he said, Behold, thou shalt see it with thine eyes, but shalt not eat thereof.... And that lord answered the man of God, and said, Now, behold, if the LORD should make windows in heaven, might such a thing be? And he said, Behold, thou shalt see it with thine eyes, but shalt not eat thereof. And so it fell out unto him: for the people trode upon him in the gate, and he died". Clearly this lord was doubting the ability of God to provide food for His people. He was not literally doubting God's ability to make literal portals in a solid firmament.

Similar symbolic language is used in Malachi 3:10 of the blessing of rain: "Bring ye all the tithes into the storehouse, that there may be meat in mine house, and prove me now herewith, saith the LORD of hosts, *if I will not open you the windows of heaven*, and pour you out a blessing, that there shall not be room enough to receive it". This is metaphorical language describing the rain as a blessing from God.

Isaiah 24:18 says that "the windows from on high are open". The context here is of God's judgment upon Israel. The previous verse says, "Fear, and the pit, and the snare, are upon thee, O inhabitant of the earth". What is being described here, in figurative language is the power of Almighty God. Verse 18 in full reads: And it shall come to pass, that he who fleeth from the noise of the fear shall fall into the pit; and he that cometh up out of the midst of the pit shall be taken in the snare: for *the windows from on high* are open, and the foundations of the earth do shake." This speaks of the authority and power of God. The record here is clearly not speaking of literal windows being opened to allow rain in from the cosmic waters above. Indeed in Isaiah 24 there is no mention of rain, but the phrase "windows on high" is used as a figure of speech.

There is therefore no support at all in the text for the assertion that clouds are "the portals through which water is released from the cosmic reservoirs". Nowhere in Scripture are "cosmic reservoirs" even hinted at, and it would seem that the only reason for suggesting such a concept is to bring the Bible into line with the mythological beliefs of the ancient near eastern civilizations. We submit that to read the text in this hyper-literal way is to lose sight of the fact that the Bible is God's Word, and He, not man, is the true Author.

The following verses clearly show that the penmen of the Bible would have known what clouds were.
*   "He bindeth up the waters in his thick clouds; and the cloud is not rent under them"[27].
*   "The clouds poured out water: the skies sent out a sound: thine arrows also went abroad"[28].
*   "If the clouds be full of rain, they empty themselves upon the earth"[29].
*   "Who can number the clouds in wisdom? Or who can stay the bottles of heaven?"[30].
*   "Yea, he ladeth the thick cloud with moisture; he spreadeth abroad the cloud of his lightning"[31].

The question for the Bible student who accepts the authority of scripture as the word of God is not, "why were these ancient people writing about clouds as windows?" but, "why *did God cause them* to use this figure of speech?" To

---

[27] Job 26:8

[28] Psalm 77:17

[29] Ecclesiastes 11:3

[30] Job 38:37

[31] Job 37:11 RV

find the answer we must compare scripture with scripture. In this case the phrase "windows of heaven" is always used in scripture to denote the power of God, and the control He has upon the affairs of men. By comparing scripture with scripture we are able to see why God caused this phrase to be used in relation to the flood account - to show us His supreme control. Causing the rains to fall is just like opening a window for the eternal Creator of the heavens and the earth.

The firmament of heaven

On the fourth creative day, God made the sun, moon and stars, and in connection with the creation of these heavenly bodies, the narrative introduces us to the "firmament of heaven": "And God said, Let there be lights in *the firmament of the heaven* to divide the day from the night; and let them be for signs, and for seasons, and for days, and years: and let them be for lights in the firmament of the heaven to give light upon the earth: and it was so. And God made two great lights; the greater light to rule the day, and the lesser light to rule the night: he made the stars also. And God set them in the firmament of the heaven to give light upon the earth, and to rule over the day and over the night, and to divide the light from the darkness: and God saw that it was good. And the evening and the morning were the fourth day" *(Genesis 1:14-19)*. We note that these heavenly bodies are said to reside, not within the heaven, but *"the firmament of the heaven"*. This is in keeping with Nehemiah's testimony that the sun, moon and stars dwell within "the heaven of heavens"[32]. This is that region beyond our atmosphere, we know as outer space.

This "firmament of heaven" is clearly a different "firmament" to the one created on day two. This becomes especially apparent when we consider the creation of the fowls of the air on the fifth creative day.

Fowl in the open firmament of heaven

Those who believe the solid dome theory of Genesis 1 lay great store by the fact that Genesis 1:20 describes the birds as flying *in front of* the *raqia*. Enns, for example, states that "according to Genesis 1:20, the birds fly in front of

---

[32] Nehemiah 9:6

the *raqia* (in the air), not in the *raqia*[33]". But this confusion has arisen because of a failure to differentiate between the heaven, and the firmament of heaven. Note what the text says: "Then God said, Let the waters abound with an abundance of living creatures, and let birds fly above the earth across the face of *the firmament of the heavens*" *(Genesis 1:20 NKJV)*. The birds are consistently described in scripture as "the fowl of heaven"[34] and they fly "in the midst of heaven"[35], but here in Genesis 1:20 they are said to fly across the face of, or in front of, "the firmament of the heavens". The Hebrew פנים - *'paniym'* - does indeed convey the idea of 'before', or 'in the face of', and this is how it appears to an observer standing upon the earth - when the birds fly in the midst of heaven, they appear to be flying *in front of the heavenly bodies* which are set in the firmament of the heavens. The careful Bible reader will conclude that the birds fly *in* the firmament created on day two called "heaven", but *in front of* the "firmament of the heavens". Neither the firmament, nor the firmament of the heavens, are solid and the text does not give us any reason to believe this.

Summary

We are now in a position to summarise our findings, illustrated in the table on the next page:

---

[33] "The firmament of Genesis 1 is solid but that's not the point". Pete Enns, *biologos.org*, Jan 14, 2010

[34] Genesis 7:23

[35] Revelation 19:17

Genesis 1	Interpretation
God	Dwells in heaven (Ecc 5:2; 1 Kings 8:43)
The firmament of the heaven	The heaven of heavens (Deut 10:14) Heavenly bodies reside here (Neh 9:6)
The waters above the firmament	The clouds (Prov 8:27-30; Psa 78:23; 108:4)
The firmament	The sky/atmosphere Birds fly here (Gen 7:23; Rev 19:17)
The waters below the firmament	Seas (Prov 8:27-30)

The diagram below will help us to visualise the arrangement.

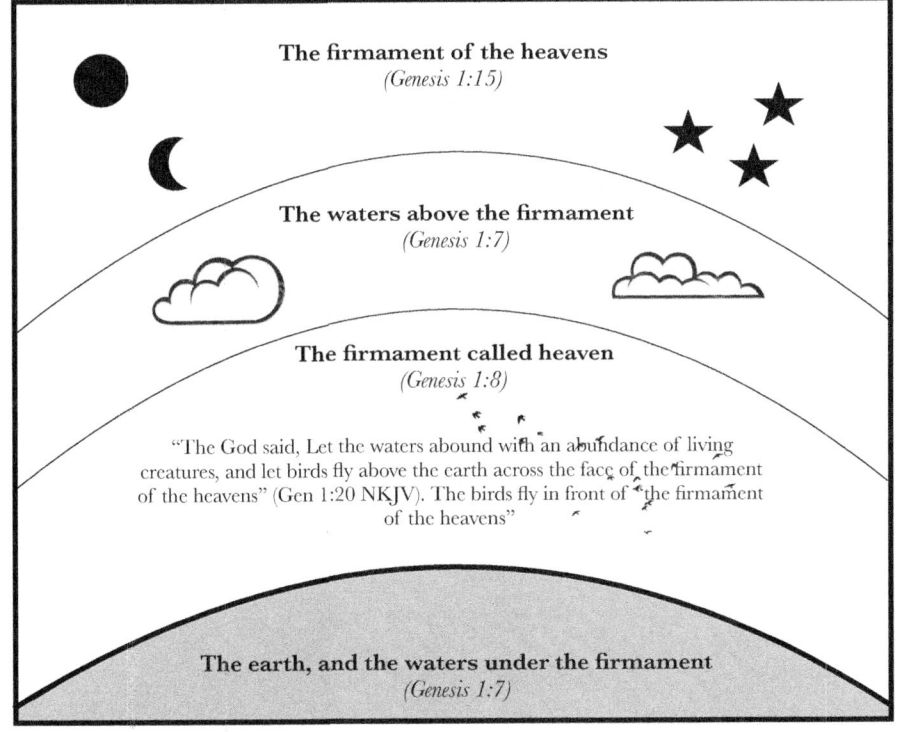

The firmament of the heavens
(Genesis 1:15)

The waters above the firmament
(Genesis 1:7)

The firmament called heaven
(Genesis 1:8)

"The God said, Let the waters abound with an abundance of living creatures, and let birds fly above the earth across the face of the firmament of the heavens" (Gen 1:20 NKJV). The birds fly in front of "the firmament of the heavens"

The earth, and the waters under the firmament
(Genesis 1:7)

This arrangement is in perfect harmony with the Psalmist's ascription of praise in Psalm 148: "Praise ye the LORD. Praise ye the LORD from the heavens: praise him in the heights. Praise ye him, all his angels: praise ye him, all his hosts. Praise ye him, sun and moon: praise him, all ye stars of light. Praise him, *ye heavens of heavens,* and *ye waters that be above the heavens.* Let them praise the name of the LORD: for he commanded, and they were created"[36]. Observe how that, according to the Psalmist, the waters are said to be "above the heavens", but the sun, moon and stars are associated with the "heaven of heavens".

It is worth observing how majestic the Psalmist's description of the cosmos is, and how different it is to the unenlightened beliefs of the ancients that we quoted in the previous chapter. This is nothing less than what we would expect since the scripture is the word of Almighty God Himself, and He created heaven and earth in the first place. The orderly arrangement of the universe is testimony to the wisdom and power of the Creator, and that wisdom is revealed to us in His word. As the Psalmist said elsewhere, "O LORD, how manifold are thy works! in wisdom hast thou made them all"[37].

---

[36] Psalm 148:1-5

[37] Psalm 104:24

5. The firmament of Genesis 1 is not solid

Part 3: Other scriptures considered

"Hast thou with him spread out the sky, which is strong, and as a molten looking glass" (Job 37:18)

Introduction

Comparing scripture with scripture, we have established that the biblical description of the firmament in Genesis 1 is perfectly compatible with modern scientific fact regarding the structure of the cosmos. The creation account has nothing to do with the supposed beliefs of the ancients, and the firmament is not presented in scripture as if it is solid.

Five other scriptures are usually advanced by the advocates of the solid dome theory of the firmament - Job 37:18, Ezekiel 1:22-28, Exodus 24:10, Isaiah 40:22 and Psalm 104:2. These will now be examined in detail, and once again it will be seen that if the scriptures are approached without preconceptions, the concept of a solid dome sky is absent.

Job 37

In Job 37, Elihu asks Job the question, "Hast thou with him spread out the sky, which is strong, and as a molten looking glass?"[1]. It is pointed out that

---

[1] Job 37:18

the Hebrew for "spread out" is רקע - *'raqa*[2], the verbal form of the Hebrew noun *'raqia'*. It is then concluded that since Elihu compares the sky to a "molten looking glass", the *raqia* must therefore be presented as being solid. In connection with this we would make the following observations:

1) Elihu invites Job to consider two elements of the sky, its *strength*, and its *resemblance to a looking glass.*

2) "Strong" is the Hebrew חזק - *'chazaq'*, and denotes the idea of mightiness. It is used, for example, in relation to the phrase "mighty hand" or "strong hand"[3], which is obviously not a reference to a literal "hard" hand but is a figure of speech representing a strong, mighty, action. It is also used in relation to a "strong west wind"[4]. We would not conclude this is speaking about the physical hardness of the wind but the mighty force of it. There is nothing in this word of itself that implies solidity. When therefore this word is used here in Job we are not to conclude that the firmament is 'solid' but rather that it denotes 'mightiness'. That the heavens are appropriately described as being mighty is clear from the following testimonies:

- "O LORD our Lord, how excellent is thy name in all the earth! Who hast set thy glory above the heavens… When I consider thy heavens, the work of thy fingers, the moon and the stars, which thou hast ordained; what is man, that thou art mindful of him? And the son of man, that thou visitest him?"[5].

---

[2] Hebrew רקע - *'raqa'*: "It can appear with a direct object, meaning "stamp down (enemies)" (2 Sam 22:43), or with an adverbial expression, meaning "Stamp (with one's feet)" (Ezek. 6:11; 25:6), with reference to a metaphorical or symbolic action. The root can also appear in participial expressions predicated of God, where it can denote God's "establishment" of the heavens (Isa. 42:5; 44:24) as well as of the earth (Psa. 136:6)". G Johannes Botterweck, Helmer Ringgren, Heinz-Joseph Fabry, *"Theological Dictionary of the Old Testament"*, Vol XIII page 647.

[3] See for example Exodus 3:19: "And I am sure that the king of Egypt will not let you go, no, not by a *mighty* hand"

[4] Exodus 10:19

[5] Psalm 8:1-4

- "The heavens declare the glory of God; and the firmament sheweth his handywork"[6].

3) "Looking glass" is the Hebrew רְאִי - *'rehee'*, which is derived from the verb רָאָה - *'raah"*, meaning 'to see'. Elihu is asking Job to compare himself with the greatness of God, who has handcrafted the sky. There are two ways of understanding what is being set forward here, both of which have nothing to do with the firmament being solid. Firstly that the heavens are "like" a looking glass in that the firmament has a semblance of luminescence, and it reflects light. It seems to almost shine in its appearance, just like a mirror appears to when one looks into it. That a mirror happens to be solid is quite beside the point. Another way to read this is that the heavens are like a looking glass in that they have been "spread out" by God[7]. In ancient times a looking glass was made of bronze metal beaten out into a thin plate until it was flat. It may be that this process of spreading out the bronze is what is being conveyed here in comparison to the creation of the heavens. In both of these ways of viewing the text, the fact that God compares the stretching out of the heavens to a *looking glass* indicates that we are intended to compare the heavens to the unique properties of a looking glass, or indeed the way it is made, and this has nothing to do with the incidental fact that a looking glass is solid.

---

6 Psalm 19:1

7 The Hebrew רָקַע - *'raqa'* - is found a total of 11 times in the Old Testament, thus: Exodus 39:3; Numbers 16:39; 2 Samuel 22:43; Job 37:18; Psalm 136:6; Isaiah 40:19; 42:5; 44:24; Jeremiah 10:9; Ezekiel 6:11; 25:6. It is used of the gold that was woven into the ephod, the censers of Korah, Dathan and Abiram that were beaten into broad plates, the enemies of David that were stamped upon as the mire of the streets and then spread abroad, the earth being stretched out, the overlaying of graven images with gold, the spreading of silver into plates, and stamping with the foot. The appearance in 2 Samuel 22:43 is particularly noteworthy in the current context: "Thou hast also given me the necks of mine enemies... Then did I beat them as small as the dust of the earth, I did stamp them as the mire of the street, and did *spread* them abroad". It makes a nonsense of the text to maintain that we are intended to conclude from this verse that David's enemies, compared to the dust of the earth, were solid! The primary meaning in all of these references is clearly that of *spreading out*.

If the idea that the *raqia* is solid is in the reader's mind beforehand, then it can easily be read into the text in Job 37:18. But there is nothing within this verse that indicates that this is its intended meaning.

Ezekiel 1 and Exodus 24

Ezekiel chapter 1 contains Ezekiel's vision of the cherubim. In verse 22 Ezekiel sees a representation of the firmament: "And the likeness of *the firmament* upon the heads of the living creature was as the colour of the terrible crystal, stretched forth over their heads above". He then sees a vision of the throne of God Himself, which is said to be above the firmament: "And above the firmament that was over their heads was the likeness of a throne, as the appearance of a sapphire stone: and upon the likeness of the throne was the likeness as the appearance of a man above upon it"[8]. The firmament is compared to "the terrible crystal", and it is maintained that this implies that the firmament is solid. This is compared with Exodus 24:10 where Moses, Aaron, Nadab and Abihu and seventy of the elders of Israel ascended mount Sinai, "And they saw the God of Israel: and there was under his feet as it were a paved work of a sapphire stone, and as it were the body of heaven in his clearness". Again, emphasis is placed on the "paved work of a sapphire stone", with its suggestion of solidity.

However:
1) Ezekiel 1 is clearly a vision. The four living creatures with wings, and the wheels full of eyes, are not to be interpreted literally, neither is the vision of the firmament.
2) In any case, there is nothing in Ezekiel 1 that suggests that the firmament is being presented as solid. It is compared with "the terrible crystal" not because crystal is solid, but because of *its colour*: "And the likeness of the firmament... was as *the colour* of the terrible crystal"[9]. "Crystal" is the Hebrew קרח - *'qerach'*, which means ice. The word is found seven times in the Old Testament, and it is variously rendered "ice" three times, "frost" three times, and "crystal" once. The point Ezekiel is making is that just as ice is transparent, so was the firmament

---

[8] Ezekiel 1:26

[9] Ezekiel 1:22

that he saw in vision. The equivalent Greek word is used of the "river of water of life" in Revelation 22:1: "And he shewed me a pure river of water of life, *clear as crystal*, proceeding out of the throne of God and of the Lamb". Are we to conclude from this that the pure river of water of life was solid, because crystal is solid? Of course not. In any case, the vision of Revelation 22 is clearly based on Ezekiel's temple vision in Ezekiel 47:5, and it is evident that the river was far from solid: "Afterward he measured a thousand; and it was a river that I could not pass over: for the waters were risen, waters to swim in, a river that could not be passed over". Neither are we intended to conclude that the firmament in Ezekiel 1, whose colour was that of the terrible crystal, was solid.

3) Exodus 24 is making the same point. Under the feet of the God of Israel Moses and his companions saw as it were "the body of heaven *in its clearness*". The Hebrew טֹהַר - 'tohar' - denotes purification, or cleansing, as can be seen from its usage in Leviticus 12:4: "And she shall then continue in the blood of her purifying three and thirty days; she shall touch no hallowed thing, nor come into the sanctuary, until the days of her *purifying* (טֹהַר) be fulfilled"[10].

4) We must bear in mind that what Moses and his fellows saw was a vision. They did not literally see "the God of Israel", because John declares that "no man hath seen God at any time"[11]. What they saw was *an angelic manifestation* of the God of Israel, because Steven tells us that Moses was "with *the angel* which spake to him in the mount Sina, and with our fathers: who received the lively oracles to give unto us"[12]. Care must be taken when seeking to extrapolate from what is clearly a vision to the Biblical description of the arrangement of the cosmos.

---

[10] See also Leviticus 12:26

[11] John 1:18

[12] Acts 7:38

5) The throne in Ezekiel 1 is *"above* the firmament"[13], but in Ezekiel 10 it is *"in* the firmament"[14]. The whole of Ezekiel's vision is a physical impossibility. He sees fantastical creatures with four faces, borne up by wheels within wheels, the height of which are dreadful. The wheels are full of eyes round about[15]. We accept that Ezekiel really did see such creatures in vision, but we are not to understand them or seek to rationalise them, in any physical, literal sense. Neither should we take Ezekiel's vision of the firmament and the throne as being in any way a guide to the composition of the literal cosmos.

6) Without wishing to labour the point, it is important to note that what Moses, Aaron, Nadab and Abihu, and the seventy elders of Israel, saw under the feet of the God of Israel was *"as it were* a paved work of a sapphire stone". It looked like a paved work of sapphire stones, but it was *not* in fact a paved work of sapphire stones. Granted they really did see something, but what they saw does not correlate with reality. We are on shaky ground when we try to use what are clearly symbolic visions to draw conclusions regarding the literal firmament of Genesis 1.

7) What Moses and his companions saw under the feet of the God of Israel was "as it were the body of heaven in his clearness". It was not heaven itself - it was clear, *like* heaven. The NIV conveys the sense well: "Under his feet was something like a pavement made of sapphire, *clear as the sky itself*".

8) It is really important that we grasp hold of the concept that just because one thing is compared to one particular aspect of something else, it does not necessarily share *all* the characteristics of the thing with which it is being compared. For example, in John's description of the one like unto the Son of man in Revelation 1:13-20, we are told that his hair was white like wool, as snow[16]. Obviously we do not conclude that his hair was wet, or freezing cold - but it was as *white* as snow. His feet were "like

---

[13] Ezekiel 1:26

[14] Ezekiel 10:1

[15] Ezekiel 1:16-19

[16] Revelation 1:14

unto fine brass"[17], but they were not made of metal. His countenance was "as the sun shineth in his strength"[18], but it was not made of incandescent gas. Similarly with the visions of Ezekiel and Exodus, under the feet of the throne was what looked like sapphire, as *clear* as the heavens. Just because a sapphire stone is solid, this does not give us liberty to conclude that the firmament is solid.

9) There is a very interesting connection between the cherubic vision of Ezekiel 1 and the vision of the heavenly throne in Revelation 4: "After this I looked, and, behold, a door was opened in heaven: and the first voice which I heard was as it were of a trumpet talking with me; which said, Come up hither, and I will shew thee things which must be hereafter. And immediately I was in the spirit: and, behold, a throne was set in heaven, and one sat on the throne....And before the throne there was *a sea of glass like unto crystal:* and in the midst of the throne, and round about the throne, were four beasts full of eyes before and behind"[19]. The firmament of Ezekiel's vision corresponds to the sea of glass, upon which the multitude of the redeemed are seen to stand[20]. This has led some to conclude that the firmament of Ezekiel's vision must be solid because John sees people standing on the sea of glass in Revelation 15. But it is important to observe that they are in different locations. In Ezekiel 1, the throne is *above* the firmament, in Ezekiel 10 the throne is *in* the firmament, but in Revelation 4:6 the sea of glass is *"before the throne"*. Careful reading of the text in Revelation reveals that what is being described is a vision of a heavenly *temple*. The record says as much in Revelation 15:5: "And after that I looked, and, behold, the temple of the tabernacle of the testimony in heaven was opened". It is based upon the tabernacle, and the temple, of the Old Testament. So

---

[17] Revelation 1:15

[18] Revelation 1:16

[19] Revelation 4:1-6

[20] Revelation 15:2

there is a door[21], seven lamps of fire corresponding to the lamp stand[22], four beasts corresponding to the cherubim[23], there are censers[24], and an altar with lifeblood poured out at its base[25], there are 24 elders corresponding to the priesthood[26], and so on. The imagery is unmistakeable. The sea of glass is clearly the counterpart to the laver - or in Solomon's temple, the "molten *sea*"[27]. Significantly, the laver of brass in the tabernacle was made by Bezaleel "of the *lookingglasses* of the women assembling, which assembled at the door of the tabernacle of the congregation"[28]. Filled with water, one of its purposes was to act as a large mirror. When a priest approached the laver, the first thing he would see would be *a reflection of himself* - and he would be pointedly reminded of his humanity, and the need for cleansing. But if he looked beyond himself, he would see something else - he would see a reflection of *heaven itself*, "which is strong, and as a molten looking glass"[29]. He would begin to dwell on the fact that in spite of his humanity God had called him to heavenly things. But - and here's the point - *the laver was not the firmament* - and neither is the sea of glass in Revelation 4.

10) Does the fact that Revelation 15:2 says that there are people standing on the sea of glass mean the firmament is solid? No, because *the laver is not the firmament*. In any case the book of Revelation is full of things that are just not literally possible - for example, four beasts within the throne, but also round about the throne, a living lamb that looked like it was slain, a

---

[21] Revelation 4:1

[22] Revelation 4:5

[23] Revelation 4:6

[24] Revelation 8:3

[25] Revelation 6:9

[26] Revelation 4:4

[27] 1 Kings 7:23

[28] Exodus 38:8

[29] Job 37:18

lamb that is also a lion, one like the Son of man holding stars in his right hand, a woman clothed with the sun, and the moon under her feet, with a crown of twelve stars, a beast with seven heads and ten horns, and so on. We have no trouble understanding that these physical impossibilities are symbols and represent something - similarly with the multitude on the sea of glass. Neither the multitude nor the sea of glass are literal.

11) The multitude are seen standing on the sea of glass in the apocalyptic vision because the Spirit is intending us to draw the conclusion that they represent the redeemed, who have been washed "with the washing of water by the word"[30]. In prospect, they have been exalted to "heavenly places in Christ Jesus"[31]. But - and here is yet another physical impossibility - the sea of glass is *mingled with fire*. That's because the multitude of the redeemed have had their faith tried by "much tribulation"[32].

When Exodus 24 and Ezekiel 1 are read with the preconceived notion of a solid firmament, this idea can be read into the text. But there is nothing within the text that demands that the firmament be understood as being solid.

Isaiah 40:22

This scripture is seeking to establish the fact that God stretched out the heavens, and spread them out: "It is he that sitteth upon the circle of the earth, and the inhabitants thereof are as grasshoppers; that stretcheth out the heavens as a curtain, and spreadeth them out as a tent to dwell in"[33]. It was as easy for Him to do this as it would be for us to put up a tent. It is not a commentary on the composition of the heavens themselves, and to read it this way is to miss the obvious point that the Spirit is using metaphorical language, and is drawing a comparison with the way a curtain is stretched out, or a tent is spread out. If it was the Spirit's intention to provide an

---

[30] Ephesians 5:26

[31] Ephesians 2:6

[32] 1 Peter 1:7

[33] Isaiah 40:22

insight into the physical composition of the heavens, we would have to assume that the Bible is saying that the heavens were made of fabric, which is clearly absurd. Further, if the writer was intending to convey the impression that the heavens were solid, with an ocean of waters above, we might well ask why such an unsuitable analogy as that of a tent, or a curtain, was chosen.

Taking such a hyper-literal approach to the text places a great strain on our understanding the other parts of the same verse, where the inhabitants of the earth are described as being "as grasshoppers". We do not suppose for one moment that the Bible intends us to understand that the inhabitants of the earth have wings and six legs! We have no difficulty in understanding the true meaning of the text, that mankind is small and almost insignificant in comparison to the Almighty Creator[34].

The imagery is clearly that of pitching a tent. The exact same imagery is found in Isaiah 54, concerning the new, heavenly Jerusalem: "Enlarge the place of thy tent, and let them *stretch forth* the curtains of thine habitations: spare not, lengthen thy cords, and strengthen thy stakes; for thou shalt break forth on the right hand and on the left; and thy seed shall inherit the Gentiles, and make the desolate cities to be inhabited"[35]. What are we to conclude from this? That the Spirit is intending us to understand that Jerusalem which is from above is solid, because a tent is solid? The very thought is absurd. We have no difficulty in identifying the fact that the Bible is using *the language of metaphor* to indicate the expansion of the heavenly Jerusalem to incorporate the Gentiles. The same is clearly the case in Isaiah 40:22. Almighty God has stretched out the heavens, like a man stretches out a tent for us to dwell under.

Psalm 104:2

The impartial reader will once again have no difficulty in identifying the language of metaphor here: "Bless the LORD, O my soul. O LORD my God, thou art very great; thou art clothed with honour and majesty. Who

---

[34] see Numbers 13:33 which confirms how this analogy is used in the scriptures

[35] Isaiah 54:2,3

coverest thyself with light as with a garment: who stretchest out the heavens like a curtain"[36]. The Psalmist is not giving us any information regarding the composition of the heavens - intentional or otherwise. Were he doing so, and intending us to infer that the comparison of the heavens with a curtain means that the heavens are solid, then logic would stipulate that we are also meant to conclude that *light is equally solid*, since it is compared to the putting on of a garment: "Who coverest thyself with light as with a garment". Once again, this hyper-literal conclusion would be absurd.

By looking at the simple context of these passages, and without approaching them with preconceived ideas, we can see that there is no foundation for the belief that the Bible is depicting a solid heaven.

Conclusion
This chapter has demonstrated that there is no substance to the notion that Genesis 1 presents the firmament as being solid. The solid dome theory is one of the main foundation arguments for those who seek to dismiss a literal understanding of Genesis 1,2. But by careful Bible reading we have seen the scriptures of truth are not based on ancient eastern pagan beliefs about the world at all. On the contrary, they are an accurate description of what has later been discovered as the correct order of things. We have come to this conclusion by simply reading the text and allowing the scriptures to interpret themselves.

The Lord God says, "The heaven is my throne, and the earth is my footstool: where is the house that ye build unto me? and where is the place of my rest? For all those things hath mine hand made, and all those things have been, saith the LORD: but to this man will I look, *even to him that is poor and of a contrite spirit, and trembleth at my word*"[37]. This is the spirit with which we must come to the word of God. We must approach it with a spirit of humility and teachableness, and we must tremble at its teaching. We must not allow our minds to be befuddled by the ideas of men. Instead, let us read the word

---

[36] Psalm 104:1,2

[37] Isaiah 66:1,2

with an open heart, and, comparing scripture with scripture, seek to understand its message.

6. What about demon possession?
Part 1: Bible demons defined

"But I say, that the things which the Gentiles sacrifice, they sacrifice to devils, and not to God: and I would not that ye should have fellowship with devils" (1 Corinthians 10:20)

Introduction

As a quick re-cap it might be worth briefly summarising what we have been looking at so far in the last three chapters. Theistic evolutionists often maintain that the Genesis account of the creation of heaven and earth reflects the unscientific beliefs of the ancients regarding the composition of the cosmos. They believed the firmament was solid, and this, it is claimed, is how the firmament is depicted in Genesis 1:6-8. Since we now know that the sky is not solid, it is argued that we are at liberty to conclude that Genesis 1 & 2 are not scientifically accurate[1]. Its purpose is not to reflect fact, and this admission allows the incorporation of other explanations of the text so that evolutionary theory can be harmonised with the Biblical record. The idea is advanced that God has *accommodated* into the Bible the worldview and understanding of the original audience - indeed this idea has been termed "Divine Accommodation".

---

[1] "Biblical literalism is an untenable exegetical option, as the view of the world it obliges a consistent exegete to hold is flatly contradicted by observable reality. The Earth is approximately 4600 million years old, orbits the sun and does not have a solid firmament overhead. Life on earth did not begin suddenly approximately 6000 years ago, but began over 3000 million years ago, and has been steadily diversifying since then." Ken Gilmore, Adapting the Biblical Discourse to Common Usage, August 23, 2012, http://berea-portal.com/adapting-the-biblical-discourse-to-common-usage/

In support of this view, it is claimed that this is not the only time that the Bible uses unscientific language.

The heart of man

One typical example that is often given[2] relates to the scripture description of the heart as the centre of thought and intellect. For example, the scriptures speak of "the thoughts of the heart"[3], "the imagination of man's heart"[4], being "meek and lowly in heart"[5], "glad of heart"[6], and "upright in heart"[7]. It is suggested that this is because the inspired writers had a primitive understanding of the heart that led them to believe that the heart was the thinking organ of the body and, for this reason, when they wrote about it they did so in a way that reflected their limited understanding. However, the Hebrew word לב - 'leb' - has a wide semantic range[8], which we today do not

---

[2] For example: "The Bible... was not written to be a scientifically accurate text book, and if we insist on interpreting certain texts that way, we risk giving our intentions for the text primacy over God's. To illustrate this point, below are some examples of what faithful people in the Bible believed, but which we now know are not scientifically accurate perspectives... In the scriptures the heart is anything but a blood pump, and as the Hebrews thought in terms of subjective experience rather than objective, scientific observation, the heart came to represent the whole being with all its physical, intellectual and psychological attributes... The ancients certainly believed these things. Those in subsequent ages believed this is what the Bible was 'clearly saying', and yet we know today these are not so. It's also worth pointing out (in case you haven't noticed it already) that God never corrected their erroneous views."
Elevating Science over God? Christadelphians Learning From Science, September 27, 2016 https://www.facebook.com/notes/christadelphians-learning-from-science/elevating-science-over-god/1543680418990810

[3] 1 Chronicles 29:18

[4] Genesis 8:21

[5] Matthew 11:29

[6] 1 Kings 8:66

[7] Psalm 97:11

[8] לב - "Inner man, mind, will, midst of things, inclinations, resolutions and determinations of the will, conscience, moral character, seat of appetites, seat of emotions and passions, seat of courage, mind, knowledge, thinking, reflection, memory" *The Brown-Driver-Briggs Hebrew and English Lexicon,* Hendrickson Publishers

necessarily appreciate when we seek to restrict its meaning to the organ of the body that is responsible for the circulation of the blood.

The truth is that the scriptures are simply using the language of metaphor, or figure of speech, as the following examples indicate:

- "Pharaoh's heart is *hardened*"[9]. God did not literally make Pharoah's heart hard. It is a figure of speech, to denote Pharoah's obstinacy.
- "I will take the *stony* heart out of their flesh, and will give them an heart of flesh"[10]. We would not suggest for one moment that the ancients believed that the heart could literally turn to stone, and we have no difficulty in understanding the Spirit to be making a comment on Israel's unbelief.
- "And it came to pass, when all the kings of the Amorites, which were on the side of Jordan westward, and all the kings of the Canaanites, which were by the sea, heard that the LORD had dried up the waters of Jordan from before the children of Israel, until we were passed over, that their heart *melted*, neither was there spirit in them any more, because of the children of Israel"[11]. It would be unreasonable to conclude from this that the writers of scripture believed that heart could literally melt.
- "And when Saul saw the host of the Philistines, he was afraid, and his heart greatly *trembled*"[12]. Similarly, the Spirit is using a figure of speech to emphasize the fact that Saul was greatly afraid of the Philistines.
- "And he also that is valiant, whose heart is as *the heart of a lion*, shall utterly melt: for all Israel knoweth that thy father is a mighty man, and they which be with him are valiant men"[13]. It would be a step too far to conclude from this that a valiant man really had a lion's heart.

---

[9] Exodus 7:14

[10] Ezekiel 11:19

[11] Joshua 5:1

[12] 1 Samuel 28:5

[13] 2 Samuel 17:10

- "And David's heart *smote him* after that he had numbered the people"[14]. Clearly this is not to be understood in any literal sense. The phrase simply conveys a sense of David's great sorrow and regret.

We have quoted at length from various scriptures to illustrate the point that we must not be blind to the simple fact that figures of speech exist in scripture, and that God connects concepts and ideas together in His word to convey certain meanings. But this is not done to reflect the limited knowledge of the ancients. God *compelled* the writers of scripture to use the particular language that they did to impart to its readers the fulness and breadth of His message. This does not mean that the writers believed in literal hearts of stone, or that hearts could melt, or tremble, or smite a person, and neither clearly do we[15].

Demon possession

The gospel accounts and the teaching of the Lord Jesus Christ regarding demons[16] and demon possession is another example often advanced of the Bible adopting concepts that do not coincide with proven scientific fact. People with mental illnesses are presented in the Gospel narratives as being possessed with demons, and since we now know that this is not in fact what was actually happening to these unfortunate individuals, the conclusion is

---

[14] 2 Samuel 24:10

[15] Even in today's scientifically advanced age with our understanding of the heart we use expressions of metaphor in relation to the heart; "my heart was in my mouth", "a matter of the heart", "his heart leapt within him" etc. We do not struggle to understand these sayings as figures of speech and not an expression of something literal.

[16] In the Authorised Version we read of the *devil,* and of *devils.* In this study we are concerned with *devils.* The original word in the Greek from which the New Testament was translated is δαιμονιον - *daimonion,* occasionally δαιμων - *daimon,* and would have been better rendered *demon.* The word δαιμονιζομαι - *daimonizomai -* occurs frequently in the New Testament and means to be possessed by a demon.
The devil is a translation of the Greek διαβολος - *diabolos,* and is not the subject of this study - here we are only concerned with demons.

drawn that the Bible is not always scientifically accurate[17]. These people with whom Jesus came into contact were not possessed by a demon, they were mentally ill.

For this reason, it is important to have clear in our minds what the Bible really teaches about demons and demon possession. When we get to grips with this fascinating subject we see that, far from reflecting the scientific ignorance of the time, the Bible is presenting a very elaborate parable concerning the disobedience of the nation of Israel, God's people, and their ultimate spiritual rehabilitation in the kingdom of God, through the work of the Lord Jesus Christ.

At the outset we want to state clearly that it cannot be denied that the Bible does sometimes use language which is not literally speaking "scientific", by virtue of the simple fact that figures of speech and poetic expressions are peppered throughout the pages of scripture. This is not in dispute here. The contention is over *the reason why*. Is it because the inspired writers were constrained by their cultural, linguistic and scientific knowledge that these expressions are found? Does the Bible accommodate the ignorance of the peoples of the cultures that it was first written to because God did not care to correct their false ideas? We do not believe so. There are specific reasons why God has chosen every word in His scriptures. By using the Bible as its own dictionary, we discover deeper lessons buried in the text. The choice of language is deliberate and is set like inter-connecting webs of ideas, to reveal hidden treasures of Divine truth to those who search. The Bible's teaching about demons makes a good case study to illustrate this.

---

[17] "Special creationists, to varying degrees, are not consistent in their Biblical literalism as they attempt to evade the fact that the Bible reflects the pre-scientific view of the world current four millennia ago. For those who believe in an inerrant Bible, the implication of scientific error in the Bible may appear threatening, hence the desperate attempt to deny the fact that a solid firmament and geocentrism really are in the Bible. The existence of a pre-scientific cosmology in the OT should however be no more threatening than *the existence of a belief in demon possession* as a cause of disease in the NT era in parts of Israel." Ken Gilmore, Adapting the Biblical Discourse to Common Usage, August 23, 2012, http://berea-portal.com

The Bible teaching about demons

The purpose of this chapter is to allow the Bible to provide its own explanation as to the nature of demons, and why people afflicted with mental illnesses were said to be possessed by them. As we seek to be guided by the word of truth[18] and not the philosophies of man, we wish to answer the question, What is it that *God* has revealed to us regarding demons? At the outset it is worth quoting a number of verses from both Old and New Testaments where, in English translations, the word "devil" appears.

- Speaking of the apostasy of the people of Israel we are told that "they sacrificed unto *devils*[19], not to God; to gods whom they knew not..."[20].

- Commanding Israel to worship the true God it was said, "They shall no more offer their sacrifices unto *devils*, after whom they have gone a whoring"[21].

- Speaking of the rebellion and unfaithfulness of Jeroboam, king of Israel, who set up an idolatrous form of worship, it was said, "He ordained him priests for the high places, and for the *devils*, and for the calves which he had made"[22].

- Of the way in which apostate Israel offered their own children as sacrifices to pagan gods the Psalmist writes, "They sacrificed their sons and their daughters unto *devils*"[23].

---

[18] 2 Timothy 2:15

[19] The Old Testament was, of course, written in Hebrew. But in the Septuagint (the ancient Greek translation of the Old Testament) the word *devils* here is δαιμονιον -*daimonion*.

[20] Deuteronomy 32:17 - the word in the Hebrew is שֵׁד - *'shed'* - meaning demon, and only used in one other place in Psalm 106:37.

[21] Leviticus 17:7 - the word for "devils" here is the Hebrew שָׂעִיר - *'sa`iyr'*. This is often translated as "goats". Some translations have translated this as "goat idols" (NIV, NLT) or "goat demons" (ESV, NASB, NET). It is translated "devils" twice.

[22] 2 Chronicles 11:15 - "devils" is again the Hebrew שָׂעִיר - *'sa`iyr'*.

[23] Psalm 106:37 - this is again the Hebrew שֵׁד - *'shed'*.

In the Old Testament then the clear, simple teaching is that *demons are the objects of pagan worship - pagan gods.* This view is also consistently upheld in the New Testament:

- Speaking of certain wicked people Revelation 9:20 says, "The rest of the men which were not killed by these plagues yet repented not of the works of their hands, that they should not worship *devils...*", showing that demons were held to be objects of worship made by mens hands, i.e. pagan gods.

- Warning the Corinthian believers that they should not continue to be involved with the idolatrous system around them, Paul writes, "Wherefore, my dearly beloved, flee from *idolatry...* the things which the Gentiles sacrifice, they sacrifice to *devils,* and not to God: and I would not that ye should have fellowship with *devils.* Ye cannot drink the cup of the Lord, and the cup of *devils:* ye cannot be partakers of the Lord's table, and of the table of *devils*"[24]. This shows that idolatry and sacrificing to devils was the same thing.

- When Paul visited the Greek city of Athens, he saw that it was "given to idolatry"[25]. When these pagans heard Paul speak about Jesus they said, "He seemeth to be a setter forth of *strange gods*"[26]. The word here translated "gods" is δαιμονιον - *'daimonion'.* The Athenians thought that in preaching Jesus, Paul was speaking about the same kind of demon-god as those which they worshipped. In the same chapter the apostle, amazed at the multitude of their gods, declared, "I perceive that in all things ye are too *superstitious*"[27]. The word he used was δεισιδαιμονεστερος - *'deisidaimonesteros',* meaning that they were extremely devoted to their demons; it was not a derogatory phrase and there is nothing to suggest that they regarded it as such. Thus again we see that demons were, to the pagans, the proper objects of their devotions.

---

[24] 1 Corinthians 10:14,20,21

[25] Acts 17:16

[26] Acts 17:18

[27] Acts 17:22

Thus consistently, in both in the Old Testament and in the New Testament, demons are spoken of in such a way as to lead us to the conclusion that *in the Bible a demon is a pagan god.* This is a key part of what God has revealed to us about demons in His word of truth, and it is entirely inconsistent with the notion of "Divine Accommodation". Clearly in these verses there is no such "accommodation" taking place at all.

Demons have no real existence

With respect to pagan gods, we can be absolutely sure of one thing - *they have no real existence.* The Bible is very clear on this matter. In Isaiah Yahweh, the true God, asks, "Is there a God beside me?" The answer comes: "There is no God; I know not any"[28]. Again the God of the Bible declares, "There is no God else beside me; a just God and a Saviour; there is none beside me. Look unto me, and be ye saved, all the ends of the earth: for I am God, and there is none else"[29].

Since the Bible declares demons to be pagan gods, and since, according to the Bible, pagan gods have no real existence, it follows that *demons do not exist.*

What about demon possession?

If demons have no real existence then it is obvious that they are unable to possess anyone. What then are we to make of such references in the Gospels as Luke 9:42, where we read about a child of whom it is said, "The devil (demon) threw him down, and tare him. And Jesus rebuked the unclean spirit, and healed the child"? How can we reconcile such accounts as this, which are not infrequent in the Gospels, with the clear teaching of the Bible that demons are pagan gods, and therefore do not exist?

To do this it is necessary to consider the way in which pagan gods were worshipped, for it was usually at pagan idol festivals that the phenomenon of "demon possession" was seen to take place. As a result of the pagan rites and devotions the spirit of the deity being worshipped was believed to take possession of the worshipper.

---

[28] Isaiah 44:8

[29] Isaiah 45:21,22

Whilst we can be absolutely sure that demons (pagan gods) do not exist in any real sense, it is equally certain that something most unusual did happen to the worshippers which convinced them that the god was taking possession of them. In fact, such things still happen today. For example, it is possible to visit West Africa and to observe ceremonies devoted to the worship of the various Voodoo deities, and to see individuals *apparently* becoming possessed by the god[30]. But these gods do not exist! What then is this observable phenomenon of "possession"?

The explanation of possession

What follows is a simplified explanation of the phenomenon of "possession". Under normal circumstances everything we see, hear or touch is received by the brain, which acts as a computer. The brain-computer then compares the new information with all other recorded experiences from the past that might have a bearing on it. To a great extent this is an automatic process not requiring conscious effort[31].

Thus, if you are informed that the moon is made of green cheese, your immediate response is, "Nonsense!" That response is the result of the brain weighing up the proposition, comparing it with certain known facts such as that cheese is made from milk, and that astronauts have been to the moon and found it to be made of rock, and then deciding that this new piece of information cannot be accepted - the moon cannot be made of green cheese. All this takes place at the subconscious level (i.e. without actually having to think it through) in a fraction of a second.

----

[30] Dr Wm. Sargant, *"The Mind Possessed"*, Heinemann, London, 1973. In this book which, because of the nature of the subject, is a somewhat distasteful production from a Christian standpoint, the author describes in detail many ceremonies visited by him personally in Africa, Brazil, Jamaica, Barbados, Haiti, the USA and elsewhere, in which demon possession phenomena were seen and many photographed.

[31] This is dealt with in greater detail by Dr Wm. Sargant, *"The Physiology of Faith"*, British Journal of Psychiatry, 1969, pp 505-18. Also his *"Battle for the Mind"*, Heinemann, London, 1957, pp1-41, is helpful. It should be noted that Sargant who rightly observed that modern "charismatic" possession of the "holy spirit" is exactly the same phenomenon wrongly proceeded to equate the modern "charismatic" experience with the New Testament outpouring of the Holy Spirit.

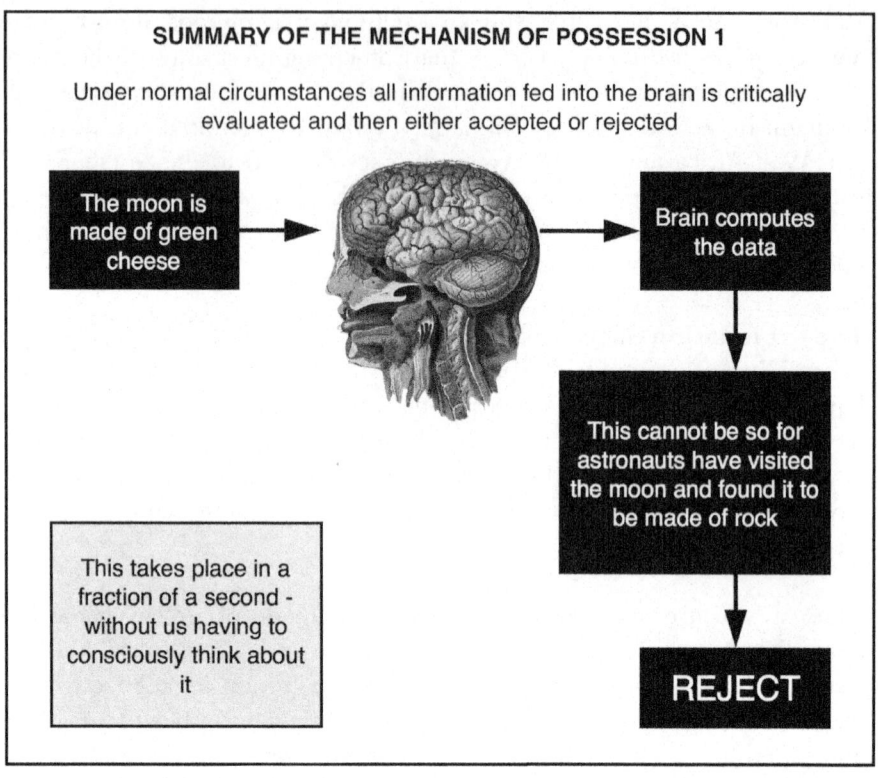

SUMMARY OF THE MECHANISM OF POSSESSION 1

Under normal circumstances all information fed into the brain is critically evaluated and then either accepted or rejected

The moon is made of green cheese

Brain computes the data

This cannot be so for astronauts have visited the moon and found it to be made of rock

This takes place in a fraction of a second - without us having to consciously think about it

REJECT

When the brain is put under great stress, changes in brain function occur that alter the way in which information is received, analysed and recorded. It is this alteration in brain function that leads to the "possession" state.

At a pagan religious festival people are put under such stress. By rhythmic clapping, drum beating and dancing, by exhaustion of the body, by inducing pain, by the use of drugs and by the employment of other more unseemly and degrading methods, the brain is progressively exhausted until the stage is reached where it no longer critically computes the information it receives. At this point any ideas fed into the brain are accepted without question. It is at this breakdown point that "possession" occurs. The individual is surrounded by the belief that possession *will* occur, and since his brain is unable to critically analyse this belief, he accepts that he *has* become possessed and behaves accordingly.

Such "possession" is usually accompanied by unconsciousness, convulsions or a trance-like state, and has been observed and described in detail by Sargant. This state of possession, which occurred at the pagan festivals in New Testament times, and which may still be seen today, is a very real and observable phenomenon. But it is not due to possession by a demon, for demons do not exist, and it can be explained physiologically - it is due to brain exhaustion, as illustrated in the diagram below.

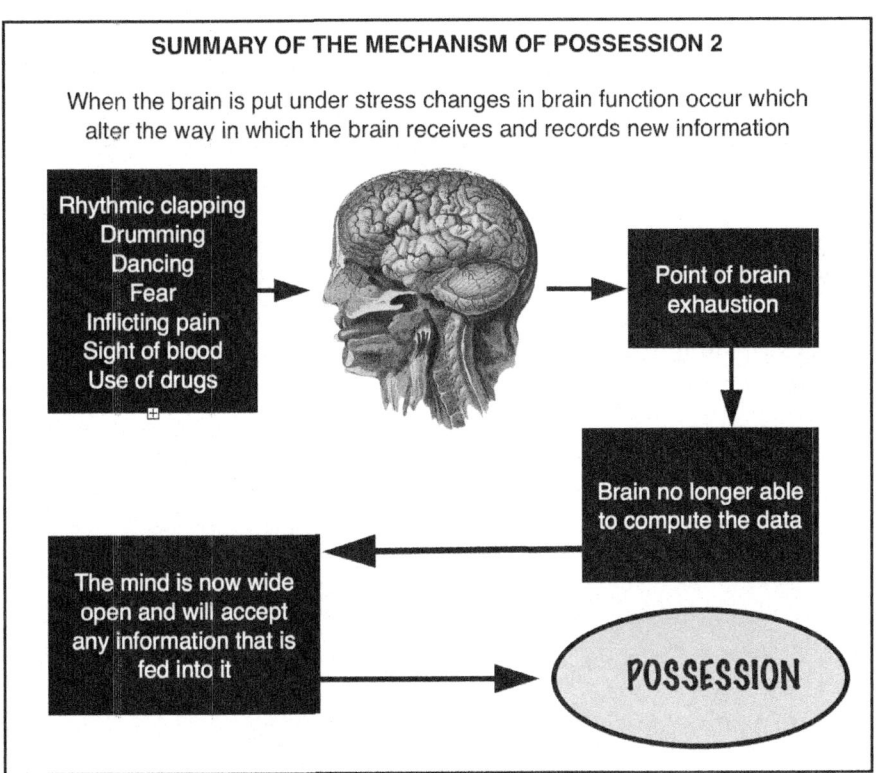

SUMMARY OF THE MECHANISM OF POSSESSION 2

When the brain is put under stress changes in brain function occur which alter the way in which the brain receives and records new information

Rhythmic clapping
Drumming
Dancing
Fear
Inflicting pain
Sight of blood
Use of drugs

Point of brain exhaustion

Brain no longer able to compute the data

The mind is now wide open and will accept any information that is fed into it

POSSESSION

Demon possession in the New Testament

With this information in mind, we may now approach the New Testament references to demon possession. In Matthew 17 a man comes to Jesus and says, "Lord, have mercy on my son: for he is a lunatic, and sore vexed: for ofttimes he falleth into the fire, and oft into the water", and we are told that "Jesus rebuked the *devil*; and he departed out of him: and the child was cured from that very hour"[32]. The child here described was subject to some kind of convulsions - in fact the Revised Version renders it, "He is an *epileptic,* and suffered grievously". But there is no suggestion that these attacks were connected in any way with a pagan religious festival. Why then attribute the convulsions to demon possession? The answer to this question provides the key to the whole problem of demon possession in the New Testament.

The only place where convulsions such as those this child exhibited were seen regularly, was at the pagan festivals[33]. There, men who were considered possessed by demons fell down in convulsion states just as this child did. How natural it was for the people in those days to assume that *the two were identical -* that the convulsions of the epileptic were due to demon possession.

Thus it was that epileptics such as this child whose convulsions resembled the convulsions of the "possession state", madness[34] which resembled the bizarre behaviour of the "possessed", and dumbness[35] with its associated vacant staring and grunting noises which resembled the trance-like states of the "possessed" at the pagan festivals, were all attributed by the common person to demons.

Demon possession and illness
The connection between demon possession and illness is beyond all reasonable doubt. Examination of the Gospel records shows that:

---

[32] Matthew 17:14,18

[33] For example the rituals of the Dionysian Mysteries "were a ritual of ancient Greece and Rome which used intoxicants and other trance-inducing techniques (like dance and music) to remove inhibitions and social constraints, liberating the individual to return to a natural state" https://en.wikipedia.org/wiki/Dionysian_Mysteries

[34] See John 10:20

[35] See Luke 11:14

1) To be possessed was equivalent to being ill

- Jesus told the twelve, "Heal the sick, cleanse the lepers, raise the dead, cast out devils"[36]. Thus the casting out of demons was a part of the healing ministry. In answer to the comment that the verse distinguishes demon possession from sickness it must be pointed out that it also distinguishes leprosy from sickness.
- In Matthew 9:32 and Luke 11:14 dumbness is said to result from demon possession.
- In Matthew 12:22 demon possession is said to cause both blindness and dumbness.
- It is clear that when the Jews used the term about Jesus they thought that he was mentally disturbed: "He hath a devil and is mad".

2) To cast out a demon was to heal an illness

- In Matthew 4:24 we are told, "They brought unto him all sick people that were taken with divers diseases and torments, and those which were possessed with devils and those which were lunatic (RV epileptic) and those that had the palsy; and he *healed* them"[37].
- Of the blind and dumb man it is said, "Then was brought unto him one possessed of a demon, blind and dumb; and he *healed* him, insomuch that the blind and dumb both spake and saw"[38].
- Of the faithful Canaanitish woman whose daughter was grievously vexed with a demon it is said, "Her daughter was *healed* from that hour"[39].

For Jesus to use such language when describing these diseases does not imply that he believed in the existence of demons - he certainly did not accept the existence of any god save his Father whom he described as "the only true

---

[36] Matthew 10:8

[37] See also Mark 3:15

[38] Also see Matthew 9:32

[39] Matthew 15:22,28 RV

God"[40]. There is no doubt he was using the commonly-understood language of his day - in fact it is difficult to see how he could do anything else other than converse with people using language that they could understand[41] [42]. But Jesus no more believed in the existence of demons as real beings causing disease than we believe men are affected by the moon when we call them *luna*-tics; or that demons are responsible for a state of confusion when we speak of pan-*demon*-ium. This is a vitally important point - whilst Jesus used the language of the day in his interactions with people afflicted with mental illness, *Jesus himself did not believe that they were possessed by demons*, because the unambiguous teaching of the Bible - both Old Testament and New Testament - is that demons are false pagan gods, and that they do not exist. It cannot be denied that Jesus would have been familiar with this aspect of Bible teaching.

Some may object that in using such language Jesus conveyed the impression that he accepted the pagan ideas about demons. To this we may say:

* Jesus did not try to counter the idea of Beelzebub ("the Lord of the flies"), but used it as an argument against the Jews[43]. If he used the idea of "the prince of the demons" which was manifestly pagan, why should he not use the current ideas of demons generally as the basis for his teaching?
* The parable of the rich man and Lazarus in Luke 16 provides further evidence that Jesus did not hesitate to use current Jewish theological ideas that had a pagan origin in his reasoning with the unbelieving

---

[40] John 17:3

[41] "Jesus had to use for the sufferer language which was helpful to him. The sufferer had been told by those around him that his trouble was demon possession. Jesus had to deal with that fact in the process of his healing work. ...It is very difficult to see what other kind of language the Lord could have used when speaking to a deluded person". Harry Tennant, *"The Christadelphians: What They Believe and Preach"* (1986), page 167

[42] See also "Demons and Demon Possession", Wrested Scriptures 2011 edition, Ron Abel and John Allfree pages 258 -275

[43] Luke 11:19

Jews[44]. But Jesus did not personally believe in the existence of a place called Abraham's bosom, or that men who died spent eternity in fiery torment.

- It is worthy of note that such demon possession as we have in the Gospels is never mentioned in the entire Old Testament period. In the New Testament demon possession is principally to be found in the synoptic Gospels with an occasional mention in the Acts of the Apostles. From this it would seem that the Almighty saw no need to instruct the Old Testament church about demon possession, neither did the Apostles in their writings see the need to instruct the New Testament ecclesias in the matter. Demon possession appears in the Gospels as a local and transitory way of speaking about certain diseases and is not a doctrine of Old Testament or New Testament belief. This being the case, it is not surprising that Jesus could accept the current way of referring to illness. A doctrine of demon possession forms no part of the Christian gospel and there is no reason why Jesus should consider it from a theological standpoint. The only reason why it is necessary for us to examine the subject today is because of the theological absurdities that have become associated with it.

Whilst we accept, therefore, that on a superficial level it would seem that Jesus on numerous occasions adopted the commonly-understood language of the day in his dealings with those afflicted with mental illnesses, and other disorders such as epilepsy, deafness and dumbness, the real question that needs to be addressed is, *Why did he do this?* It is not good enough simply to say that he was acquiescing to the mistaken beliefs of the day, since we have seen that the scriptures - both Old Testament and New Testament - are unambiguous in their testimony that demons are pagan gods, and that they have no real existence, which Jesus knew full well. There is a profound reason why Jesus framed his teaching in these terms, and this will be explored in the next chapter.

---

[44] See Josephus' "Discourse to the Greeks Concerning Hades", Whiston's Josephus, Pickering & Inglis Ltd. 1964, page 637.

7. What about demon possession?
Part 2: The reason for demon possession in the New Testament

"And they come to Jesus, and see him that was possessed with the devil, and had the legion, sitting, and clothed, and in his right mind: and they were afraid" (Mark 5:15)

Questions to be answered

There must be a reason why Jesus chose to use the commonly accepted language of the day concerning demons, and demon possession, in spite of the plain fact that elsewhere in the Bible it is clearly taught that demons are pagan gods that have no real existence. Jesus knew this, and yet still he deliberately chose to speak about demons. Why did he do this? Not only did Jesus himself use this language but the divinely inspired[1] writers used this language too[2]. Why did God cause His word to be penned in such a way? This is the real question that is addressed in this chapter.

One possible reason may well lie in God's attitude towards Israel at the time of Jesus' ministry. In Isaiah 6, which is a prophecy about Jesus, it is said, "Go and tell this people, Hear ye indeed, *but understand not;* and see ye indeed, *but perceive not.* Make the heart of this people fat, and make their ears heavy, and shut their eyes; lest they see with their eyes, and hear with their ears, and

---

[1] 2 Timothy 3:16, 2 Peter 1:21

[2] See for example Mark 1:32,34,39 which all, by way of commentary, reference "devils" being cast out.

understand with their heart, and convert, and be healed"[3]. To use the language of the day about demons was one of the ways of "shutting their eyes". The truth was being presented in such a way that only those who had ears to hear would take the trouble to grasp the truth of Divine teaching.

That said, one cannot help but think that there must be more to the use of the language of demonology in the scriptures than simply this. It is a curious thing that there is no reference *throughout the entire Old Testament* to diseases being connected with demons. It is only in the ministry of Jesus and very occasionally during the early labours of the apostles that we read of certain diseases being attributable to demons. In fact, so frequent are the references to demon possession in the ministry of Jesus that we could be forgiven for thinking that the Gospels are preoccupied with the subject. Why is this?

To answer this question, we must consider two methods of instruction used by Jesus in his ministry - parables and miracles. It may come as a surprise to learn that the miracles were designed to instruct, but we hope to show that this was indeed the case.

The parables

The spoken words of Jesus were always purposeful and full of meaning. They were, in fact, words received from his Father, for "he whom God hath sent speaketh the words of God"[4], and again, "He that sent me is true; and I speak to the world those things which I have heard of him... as my Father hath taught me, I speak these things"[5].

When he spoke the parables there was nothing haphazard about them; there was always a reason why he spoke a particular parable. Thus, for example, the parable of the sower in Luke 8:4-15 was given to illustrate the different responses in Israel to his teaching, and the parable of the vineyard in Matthew 21:33-46 represented the attitude of Israel's leaders to the work of

---

[3] Isaiah 6:9,10. See also John 12:37-41

[4] John 3:34

[5] John 8:26,28

God through him. To understand the parables it is necessary to interpret them. This is often straightforward as in the parable of the sower, but it sometimes proves to be a most difficult exercise. One such difficult parable is found in Matthew 12:43-45: "When the unclean spirit[6] is gone out of a man, he walketh through dry places, seeking rest, and findeth none. Then he saith, I will return into my house from whence I came out; and when he is come, he findeth it empty, swept, and garnished. Then goeth he, and taketh with himself seven other spirits more wicked than himself, and they enter in and dwell there: and the last state of that man is worse than the first. Even so shall it be also unto this wicked generation".

Whatever the detailed explanation of the parable might be, the inescapable "punch line" of the parable, which comes in the final sentence, is that Jesus would have us view the Jewish nation at that time in their history as being like a demon-possessed man - "Even so shall it be also unto *this wicked generation*".

The casting out of the demon in the first place probably has reference to the work of John the Baptist, whose preaching met with a great response: "There went out unto him all the land of Judaea, and they of Jerusalem, and were all baptized of him in the river of Jordan, confessing their sins"[7]. Even the Pharisees and the Sadducees came to him, although he rebuked them[8]. But the repentance was short-lived, and when Jesus came to them they had returned to their old ways and, rejecting both him and his teaching, they crucified him. Thus the last state of Israel was worse than the first. But, whatever the correct interpretation of the parable might be, the point to be emphasized is that in this parable Jesus spoke of *the nation of Israel* as being like a demon-possessed man.

---

[6] In this parable the word "demon" is not used. But that demons and unclean spirits are identical is clear from such passages as Mark 5:12,13; Luke 4:33 etc.

[7] Mark 1:5

[8] Matthew 3:7

The miracles

Just as the parables of Jesus were the *words* of God through His Son, so the miracles of Jesus were the *works* of God. Thus he said, "The works which the Father hath given me to finish, the same works that I do, bear witness of me, that the Father hath sent me"[9]. And again, "I must work the works of him that sent me"[10]. As with the words so with the works - they were purposeful and appropriate to the circumstances in which they were performed. Thus the healing of the man with the withered hand[11] was not performed simply because Jesus felt sorry for the man, but in order to establish his teaching concerning the sabbath day. The cursing of the fig tree[12] was really an enacted parable in which Jesus was conveying to his disciples an important message about the nation of Israel. Israel was the fig tree which had leaves but no fruit. Because Israel had failed to bring forth the fruit of righteousness before God it was cursed as a nation[13].

In a similar way the miracles of Jesus that had to do with the casting out of demons were intended to teach the disciples something about the nation of Israel, for we have already seen from the parable of the man with the unclean spirit that Jesus wanted them to view that "wicked generation" as demon-possessed.

What a fitting representation this was. God had predicted through Moses that Israel would forsake Him and turn aside "to devils (i.e. demons), and not to God, to gods whom they knew not, to new gods that came newly up..."[14]. This was precisely the situation at the time of Jesus. They had turned aside to the foolish superstitions of the Gentile world and had embraced ideas and

----

[9] John 5:36

[10] John 9:4

[11] Luke 6:8-10

[12] Matthew 21:19,20

[13] Compare Luke 13:7-9

[14] Deuteronomy 32:17

forms of worship that were opposed to God's truth[15]. The pagan ideas of the Gentiles had entered into the body politic of Israel - Israel had become possessed of the pagan demons. Thus the nation was fittingly represented by a madman or an epileptic which, according to the superstitions of the day, were illnesses due to demon possession. This lies at the root of the teaching of Jesus with the demoniacs.

Nowhere is this more clearly seen than in the miracle of the healing of the Gadarene demoniac, which we shall now consider.

The madman of Gadara *(Mark 5:11-20)*

It would be possible to write an extensive treatise on the wonderful way in which Jesus employs this miracle in order to highlight some of the important Old Testament prophetic teaching about the nation of Israel, but one or two points must suffice.

- The man is clearly insane, for when he was healed he was said to be "in his right mind"[16]. This is a fitting representation of the nation of Israel which, because of its turning aside after the demon gods, was to be nationally smitten with madness[17].
- The man is introduced as "having his dwelling among the tombs"[18], which is very reminiscent of Isaiah's prophetic picture of apostate Israel - "a people that provoketh me to anger continually[19] ... which remain *among the graves* and lodge in the monuments"[20]. Isaiah proceeds to speak of Israel "eating swine's flesh" which was forbidden by God's law. The

---

[15] Under the heading "Beelzebub, lord of the fly", Young's Concordance states, "A heathen deity to whom the Jews ascribed supremacy among evil spirits" - which is of course confirmed by Matthew 12:24.

[16] Mark 5:15

[17] See Deuteronomy 32:16, and compare Deuteronomy 28:28

[18] Mark 5:3

[19] The keen student will note that in this description of Israel that "provoketh me to anger" there is a reference by Isaiah back to Deuteronomy 32:16 where it was prophesied that Israel would provoke God to anger with their demons.

[20] Isaiah 65:3,4

reference to the herd of swine in the miracle is surely no mere coincidence.

- The man, then, represents apostate Israel defiled by contact with Gentile abominations. But it is Israel at a particular time in history. This comes over more clearly in the Revised Version: "No man could *any more* bind him, no, not with chains"[21]. The man had been bound in the past but the time had arrived when it was no longer possible to bind him. Like this madman Israel has been repeatedly bound in the past. For example, the nation was led captive by the Babylonians in Old Testament times and again by the Romans in AD 70. But the people of Israel have been preserved and today are being regathered. The State of Israel was re-established in 1948 and the time will come when, says God, "I will break his (i.e. the Gentile) yoke from off thy neck, and will burst thy *bonds*, and strangers shall *no more* serve themselves of him"[22]. Thus the man is a fitting representation of Israel - apostate Israel - at the time of the restoration but just before the manifestation of Jesus as Messiah at his second coming.

- Jesus will appear to Israel and will provide the nation with the means of forgiveness and cleansing. When Jesus confronted the demoniac the latter asked, "What have I to do with thee, Jesus, thou son of the most high

---

[21] Mark 5:3 RV

[22] Jeremiah 30:8

God?"[23] He was not particularly pleased to see Jesus. So, too, it would appear that Israel will not be eager to part with her Gentile ways and superstitions. But God has spoken; Israel will be cleansed - "I will cut off the names of the *idols* out of the land... I will cause... *the unclean spirit* to pass out of the land"[24]. In the miracle this is acted out when the demons (unreal and therefore invisible) become identified with the swine (forbidden by the law and therefore a visible symbol of Israel's sin), which then ran headlong down the cliff and perished in the sea. Thus in a most amazing way was enacted the future cleansing work of Jesus with Israel, of which the prophet speaks when he predicted, "Thou wilt cast all their sins *into the depths of the sea*'[25].

- The man sitting, clothed, and in his right mind, free from his chains, rid of his unclean spirit and delivered from the graves reminds us of Isaiah's picture of Israel's future glory: "Put on thy strength, O Zion, put on *thy beautiful garments*, O Jerusalem, the holy city: for henceforth there shall no more come into thee the uncircumcised and the *unclean*. Shake thyself from the dust, *arise*, and *sit down*, O Jerusalem: loose thyself from the

---

[23] It is sometimes asked, is not the real existence of demons proved by James' statement, "The devils also believe and tremble" (James 2:19)? James no doubt is referring to such events as this in Mark 5 where clearly the demon possessed man was afraid of Jesus (see the parallel record in Matthew 8:29) whom he proclaimed to be the "Son of the most high God" (Mark 5:7). He thus both believed and trembled. The following points may be helpful:

a) There is frequently employed in the Bible a figure of speech where one name or noun is used instead of another, E.g. Job 32:7: "Days should speak, and multitude of years should teach wisdom". In this verse clearly "days" means"men who have days", and "years" means "men who have years". By the same figure, in "devils also believe and tremble", devils stands for "men who have devils".

b) Luke 11:14 says, "Jesus was casting out a devil and it was dumb". Here the demon is said to be dumb but in fact it was the man who was dumb, for "when the devil had gone out the dumb spake".

c) Luke 4:41 reads, "Demons also came out of many, crying out and saying, Thou art the Christ the Son of God". Again, bearing in mind the above, a common sense reading of the passage is that when the demons were cast out, the people declared Jesus to be the Son of God.

[24] Zechariah 13:2

[25] Micah 7:19

bands of thy neck, O captive daughter of Zion"[26]. The "right mind" is also described by the prophet in the same chapter when he proceeds to say, "My people *shall know* my name... they *shall know* in that day that I am he"[27].

Thus in a most remarkable way Jesus in this miracle presents, in the form of an enacted parable, the wonderful message of the Old Testament regarding God's purpose with Israel[28].

It is not therefore enough to say that the writers of scripture used the language of the day because they were limited by their own knowledge or world view. Neither is it good enough to simply assume that God has accommodated man's error into His word. *God* has chosen the words which have become all the scriptures of truth. These words and concepts all interlink to teach us the wonderful and humbling lesson of the evils of idolatry whilst at the same time recording historical facts. This brings out a deeper appreciation of the teaching that lies behind the "works" recorded.

The historicity of the miracles

We might make one final point. Some theistic evolutionists, after unfortunately and unnecessarily concluding that the Bible uses primitive and scientifically mistaken concepts (such as demon possession), continue one step further and maintain that therefore the Genesis account of creation need not be taken as an account of historical fact. Such a conclusion is not valid. Even

---

[26] Isaiah 52:1,2

[27] Isaiah 52:6

[28] The healing of the man's son in Matthew 17 has a similar message. The following "clues" will enable the student to seek this out:
a) "My son" (verse 15) - compare with "Israel is my son..." (Exodus 4:22).
b) "Falleth into the fire and oft into the water" - compare with Isaiah 43:2: "When thou passest through the waters, I will be with thee... when thou walkest through the fire, thou shalt not be burned".
c) Israel, God's son, has "fallen" successively before Assyria, Babylon, Rome and so throughout history. But the fire and the water have not destroyed the people and their ultimate healing at the hand of their Messiah is assured. They will then be "cleansed from all your idols" (demons), and in place of this unclean spirit "a new spirit will I put within you" (Ezekiel 36:25,26).

if it is assumed (we believe wrongly) that Jesus and the inspired narrators used erroneous ideas and the language of the time in the Gospels because they were limited by the knowledge of their day, this clearly does not give us liberty to conclude that the actual historical events being described did not take place. We cannot dismiss the miracles as poetic stories with no basis in historical fact, simply on the ground that the narrative of the miracles uses terminology that is deemed to be "unscientific". The logical end-point of this reasoning would be that Jesus did not, in fact, heal the Gadarene demoniac at all, since the account uses an unscientific depiction of the man's illness. This would then call into question the whole of the Gospel accounts of the work and ministry of the Lord Jesus Christ, and take away the power and wonder of the miracles Jesus performed.

Yet this is precisely what we are being encouraged to do with the creation account in Genesis - to dismiss the idea that the 6 day creation of the heavens and earth in Genesis 1 and 2 was an actual historical event, because it uses language which, according to some, is not in accordance with scientific fact[29]. Such an underestimation of the power and majesty of the revelation of God's word is not, we submit, in keeping with the spirit of Isaiah 66:2: "...to this man will I look, even to him that is poor and of a contrite spirit, *and trembleth at my word."*

Summary

* Demons in the Bible are pagan deities.
* Demon possession was a phenomenon that was frequently seen at pagan festivals when those "possessed" became unconscious, had convulsions or passed into trance-like states. This same phenomenon can be observed today in primitive civilizations and it can be readily explained in scientific, physiological terms.
* Epilepsy, various forms of mental illness and dumbness, resemble the so-called "possession state", and were considered by the contemporaries of

---

[29] "...the Bible was given to people who were not scientifically literate, and therefore was intended not to provide scientifically accurate information that the people of Israel would not understand, but rather to point out that God was the creator of the universe." Ken Gilmore, Adapting the Biblical Discourse to Common Usage, August 23, 2012, http://berea-portal.com/adapting-the-biblical-discourse-to-common-usage/

Jesus to be the same phenomenon, and were therefore attributed to demon possession.

- Jesus adopted this way of speaking about certain illnesses and, by parable and miracle, represented apostate Israel as a demon possessed man[30].

- His miracles, which were frequently enacted parables, developed this idea in a most detailed way. Israel was (and is) like a demon possessed man and God's purpose is that the nation will be healed and made sane by Jesus when he returns to rule over them. This will be a day of great blessing for the Gentile nations also, for the purpose of God is that the influence of Jesus will ultimately become world-wide. Then ideas such as demon possession will be cast aside, for "the Gentiles shall come unto thee from the ends of the earth, and shall say, Surely our fathers have inherited lies, vanity, and things wherein there is no profit"[31].

- Jesus himself, and the writers of the New Testament, clearly understood and believed that demons do not exist and therefore that they do not possess a man.

- The Lord's use of demon language bears *no resemblance whatsoever* to the suggestion made by theistic evolutionists that parts of the Bible do not accord with scientific fact *because* the men writing it were constrained by their primitive and mistaken knowledge. Rather there was reason and purpose behind the Lord's teaching, and his use of demon terminology.

- Therefore the Biblical teaching about demons gives *no support* to the notion that the Bible, and in particular the book of Genesis, is scientifically inaccurate, and that Genesis 1 and 2 can be dismissed as a true and factual account of the creation of heaven and earth.

---

[30] An argument sometimes advanced for the real existence of demons is that it is said that "the devils departed" out of the possessed (e.g. Luke 8:35), implying that they were real beings. However, this does not in any way imply personality of the demons for it is also said, "The fever left her" (Mark 1:31), and "the leprosy departed" (Mark 1:42). Neither fever nor leprosy have any personal existence. Also it is argued by some that since Jesus spoke to the demons this proves that they must have existed in a personal sense. But in Luke 4:39 Jesus "rebuked the fever…", and in Mark 4:39 he "rebuked the wind, and said to the sea…". None would see the need to insist that the fever, the wind or the sea had real personality.

[31] Jeremiah 16:19

8. The historical Adam

"And so it is written, The first man Adam was made a living soul; the last Adam was made a quickening spirit" (1 Corinthians 15:45)

Introduction

The theistic evolutionists put forward a number of differing viewpoints regarding the biblical Adam, none of which are consistent with the simple teaching of the scriptures.

At the extreme end of the spectrum, some theistic evolutionists maintain that Adam was not a real historical person at all, but he should be viewed as an archetypal figure, and that what is important is that we look at the "Adam" within ourselves[1]. According to this perspective, it is an unnecessary detail to insist on a real historical Adam since it has no bearing on the fundamental Gospel of salvation. The foundation of our faith is not Adam, but Jesus Christ. This view completely dismisses the belief that Genesis is recording literal historical events, and paves the way for the acceptance of evolutionary theory regarding the origin of life.

Some theistic evolutionists do believe that Adam was a real historical individual, but it is consistently maintained that he was not the *first* man - there was a race of pre-Adamic human-like creatures that arose by the

---

[1] https://biologos.org/blogs/archive/series/was-adam-a-real-person

process of evolution[2], and this is where it is supposed that Cain got his wife from. As far as the origin of Adam is concerned, the opinion of theistic evolutionists is further divided. Some believe that Adam was a special creation of God in the Near East about 6,000 years ago, whilst others claim that he was in fact one of the evolved human-like beings, perhaps a farmer who lived about 200,000 years ago in Africa, and he represented the first one with whom God could "do business"[3].

Fundamental to these varying points of view is the belief that Genesis 1 and Genesis 2 represent two separate creation stories[4], but even here there is divergence of opinion. Some will say that neither Genesis 1 nor Genesis 2 represent historical fact, but should be viewed simply as two teaching stories with different points of emphasis, in the genre of other Ancient Near East literature. Others suggest that Genesis 1 is not historical, and has to be harmonised with current evolutionary thinking, and in particular Genesis 1:26,27 relates to the evolutionary development of a human-like race over millions of years, whilst Genesis 2 is historical and deals specifically with the special creation of Adam.

The question as to whether Genesis 1 and Genesis 2 are two separate creation stories will be dealt with at length in chapters 11 and 12. We simply point out at this stage that this is an interpretation that is entirely without foundation. Genesis 1 and 2 are two historical accounts of the same creative work of God[5], with differences of emphasis. Genesis 1 considers the whole

---

[2] This is not a new view in Christadelphian circles. In 1964 Ralph Lovelock at Watford, UK, put forward this idea in his studies entitled "The Origin of Man". After a prolonged period of discussion withhim, the Arranging Committee at Watford took the decision to withdraw fellowship from him, and they published a report and a statement outlining their reasons why. In fact, as early as 1888, the idea that there was a race of hominids existing at the same time as Adam was refuted in the Christadelphian Magazine by Frank Shuttleworth in two short articles, both of which are well worth reading: "The First Man", *The Christadelphian Magazine,* 1888, Vol 25, pp 618-619; 679-681.

[3] https://biologos.org/blogs/archive/adam-and-eve-literal-or-literary

[4] https://biologos.org/blogs/archive/series/israels-two-creation-stories

[5] For more information on this see "Jesus' reading of Genesis 1-2", Peter Heavyside, *Testimony,* September 2015, 353-355.

of God's creative work, whereas Genesis 2 focuses on the creation of man, and his placement in the garden of Eden.

Objectives

The purpose of this chapter is to establish the importance of accepting the existence of Adam as a real historical individual, and that Genesis 1:26,27 and Genesis 2:7 relate to the specific creation of Adam. In chapter 9 we shall demonstrate that it is not consistent with the teaching of the rest of scripture to maintain that Adam was not the first man, or that there was a race of human-like creatures contemporary with Adam.

At the outset, we need to have very clear in our minds that, of the alternative views regarding Adam summarised above, *none of them are taught, or even hinted at, in the Bible.* It appears that these views have been arrived at as a result of the desire to seek to harmonise Bible teaching with the so-called "evidence" of science in general, and the theory of evolution in particular.

Adam was a real person

We begin with the question regarding Adam's historicity. Does the Bible give us any indication that Adam should be viewed as anything other than a real, historical human being who lived some 6,000 years ago? The answer to this question is an unequivocal "No", as we shall seek to demonstrate.

Adam outside of Genesis

Outside the book of Genesis, Adam is mentioned by name a total of twelve times[6]. In all of these occurrences, the historicity of Adam is taken absolutely for granted. Job who, it is generally accepted, lived in patriarchal times, clearly believed in his existence, and accepted the fact that Adam transgressed, and sought to cover his nakedness: "If I covered my transgressions *as Adam*, by hiding mine iniquity in my bosom"[7]. Adam is mentioned in the genealogy of 1 Chronicles 1:1, and also, most importantly, in the genealogy of the Lord Jesus Christ in Luke 3:38. If doubt is cast upon

---

[6] Deuteronomy 32:8; 1 Chronicles 1:1; Job 31:33; Hosea 6:7; Luke 3:38; Romans 5:14; 1 Corinthians 15:22,45; 1 Timothy 2:13,14, Jude v 14

[7] Job 31:33

the existence of Adam, then logic would dictate that equal doubt should also be cast upon any or all of Adam's descendants, and this ultimately includes Jesus himself. Yet there is absolute consistency between the genealogy outlined in Genesis 5, 1 Chronicles 1:1-4 and Luke 3:36-38. Similarly, Jude in his epistle states with authority that Enoch was "the seventh from Adam"[8].

Eve the mother of all living

Genesis 3:20 tells us that "Adam called his wife's name Eve; *because she was the mother of all living*". Whilst we accept that there is a spiritual aspect to Adam's naming of his wife, namely that eternal life would be made available to all who form an association with the woman's seed, nevertheless the *spiritual* lesson must necessarily arise out of the *natural*, that Eve was in reality the mother of all living[9]. If there was a race of evolved human-like creatures contemporary with Adam, then this was not the case. Even if we suppose that Adam was a special creation of God, and in the seclusion of the garden of Eden was unaware of the existence of human-like beings elsewhere, it is inadmissible that the inspired writer of the book of Genesis would not seek to correct Adam's misconception, or even that another inspired writer would not give us a fuller picture to clarify the situation. As no correction or clarification has been made we must take this to mean what it says, that Eve indeed was the mother of *all* of the human race.

The Apostolic perspective

The inspired apostle Paul[10] gives the explicit statement that "Adam was first formed, then Eve. And Adam was not deceived, but the woman being deceived was in the transgression"[11]. Clearly the apostle believed not only in the existence of Adam, but also Eve, and there is no reason whatsoever to

---

[8] Jude v 14

[9] "This is true literally, but it also has a figurative significance. Eve represents the bride of Christ, the Ecclesia associated with the Covenant of promise, "the mother of us all" (Gal 4:26). They are truly "living ones" who are of the multitudinous seed of the woman; the others are "dead in trespasses and sins" (Eph 2:1)". H P Mansfield, *The Christadelphian Expositor Series - Genesis,* page 90, Logos Publications.

[10] 1 Corinthians 7:40

[11] 1 Timothy 2:13,14

take these words of Paul at anything other than face value. Also he accepted without question that they were both "formed" - in keeping with the testimony of Genesis 2:7 that "the LORD God *formed* man of the dust of the ground, and breathed into his nostrils the breath of life; and man became a living soul". Paul did not question the Genesis account of the fall from grace, and that as a result of the sin of one man "death passed upon all men", such that "death reigned from Adam to Moses"[12]. The teaching of Paul regarding the atonement, the cornerstone of faith, is argued from this very basis that Adam, by disobedience to the Divine commandment, was condemned to return to the dust of the ground from whence he came, and needed salvation from sin and death. We shall look at this in more detail in the next chapter.

Salvation from the consequences of Adam's sin has been secured by the Lord Jesus Christ - a real descendant of Adam according to the genealogy of Luke 3:23-38. It is worthy of note that Luke 3 is also consistent with the Genesis account in stating that Adam was "the son of God". Neither of these accounts even suggest that Adam might have descended from another being.

Jesus is described as "the last Adam" in 1 Corinthians 15:45: "And so it is written, The first man Adam was made a living soul; *the last Adam* was made a quickening spirit". We note here that the apostle, through inspiration, is drawing a contrast between Adam, whom he describes as "the first man", and Jesus Christ himself. Adam was "made a living soul", but Christ "a quickening (or life-giving) spirit". We would not question for one moment that Christ was indeed made "a quickening spirit" after his resurrection from the dead, and if Adam was not literally made "a living soul" the force of the comparison is lost.

It may be objected that Christ was not literally "the last Adam", so why do we necessarily have to understand "the first Adam" as being confirmation that Adam really was the first man? To say this is to fail to perceive that Paul is using Adam and Christ as *two federal heads*. We are either "in Adam", or "in Christ"[13] - there is no other choice. Adam and Christ were both sons of God,

---

[12] Romans 5:12,14

[13] 1 Corinthians 15:22

and both special creations of God, and in this sense they are unique. Adam was the first specially created son of God, and Christ was the last. In comparing Adam with Christ, Paul says: "For as in Adam all die, even so in Christ shall all be made alive"[14]. What is the point of the comparison between Adam and Christ, if Adam was fictitious? Furthermore, if Adam is fictitious, it cannot be true that all in Adam "die" - the death "in Adam" must be fictitious too - yet we know from experience that all of Adam's offspring really do die. The comparison with being "made alive" in Christ becomes completely lost if Adam never existed[15].

On Mars' hill the apostle Paul declared that God "giveth to all life, and breath, and all things; *and he made of one every nation of men* for to dwell on all the face of the earth, having determined their appointed seasons, and the bounds of their habitation"[16]. Paul believed and unambiguously stated that all nations of men were made "of one". If the beliefs of theistic evolutionists are to be accepted, then we have to admit that what the apostle says here is not true.

Paul was conversing on this occasion with the great philosophers and academics of his day, some of whom held beliefs similar to modern evolutionary thought. If there was ever a time when Paul would have been expected to cast doubt on the origin of all nations from one man, this was it. But he did not do so. He held to the view plainly set out in the rest of scripture, that human kind descended from Adam.

Were they all mistaken?

If we maintain that Adam was not a historical person, then we would have to conclude that Moses, Job, the Chronicles genealogy, Hosea, Luke, Paul and Jude were either mistaken, or were speaking of things as if they were

---

[14] ibid

[15] "There can be no doubt that in the mind of Paul Christ was a real person whom he had seen; it cannot reasonably be doubted that for him Adam was no less real as a historical character. On this depends all his reasoning on the significance of being "in Adam" and "in Christ"" The Christadelphian Vol. 104, *Paul's Use of the Scriptures*, L. G. Sargent. May, 1967

[16] Acts 17:25,26 RV

historical fact when in reality they were simply allegorical stories with no basis in fact. We would have to accept that the process of Divine inspiration has allowed for error to creep into the text.

This is not to say that the Divine text never uses the language of allegory, or figure of speech as a literary device - of course it does. The previous chapters on demon possession have illustrated that this is so. But in such cases there is always a *textual reason* for the use of such language (e.g. to direct us back to the Old Testament to uncover the deeper meaning of the miracles). The suggestion that Adam is not the first man calls into question the clear and unambiguous scripture passages, outlined above, where there are no obvious textual reasons for doubting the literal historicity of the account. This is not consistent with the claim of scripture that "all scripture is given by inspiration of God"[17], and that God is "a God of truth"[18] who "cannot lie"[19].

Is believing in Adam necessary?

Let us, for the sake of argument, assume that it is not necessary for the believer in Christ to accept the existence of a literal, historical Adam. We would then be at liberty to deny the existence of Eve, since she was supposedly made out of Adam's side. The record of Genesis 2 indicates that God planted a garden eastward in Eden, "and the LORD God took the man, and put him into the garden of Eden to dress it and to keep it"[20]. But if Adam did not exist we may dismiss the existence of the garden of Eden, and therefore also the tree of life, and the tree of knowledge that were supposedly planted in the midst of the garden. Similarly, if Eve was not a real historical person, then the conversation between Eve and the serpent did not really take place. Neither is it necessary to believe that Eve partook of the forbidden fruit, because she did not exist. We can also discount God's conversation with Adam, Eve or the serpent, in the garden, and this includes

---

[17] 2 Timothy 3:16

[18] Deuteronomy 32:4

[19] Titus 1:2

[20] Genesis 2:15

the words of God concerning the enmity between the serpent and the seed of the woman in Genesis 3:15: "And I will put enmity between thee and the woman, and between thy seed and her seed; it shall bruise thy head, and thou shalt bruise his heel". This is the first Biblical promise concerning the coming of a Saviour who would overcome the problem of sin, that found its fulfilment in the Lord Jesus Christ, and we would have to conclude this was not a real promise given at a real point in time since those to whom it was "spoken" did not exist.

What this illustrates is that the whole of the Genesis account stands or falls together, and if one part is dismissed as not historical fact, the rest can follow. Then Abraham, Isaac and Jacob need not necessarily be considered as literally being the fathers of the nation of Israel, and the covenants God made with them - described by Paul as "the gospel"[21] - may be disregarded. Similarly the account of Joseph, Israel's development into a nation in Egypt, and indeed all other key accounts in Genesis that form the basis for many of the themes that emerge later in scripture, may be dismissed. But more even than that - the integrity of all "holy men of God" who make reference to the Eden account throughout scripture is called into question. Thus little by little the whole of the Gospel of salvation loses its foundation and becomes baseless[22], and the foundation principle of Divine inspiration loses all authority. Some who have accepted the arguments of theistic evolution have taken things to such an extreme that nothing in Genesis 1-11 is accepted as literal historical fact, and sadly this, in some cases, has led to the total loss of faith[23].

---

[21] Galatians 3:8

[22] It is probable that this is one of the reasons that a literal view of a historical Adam is referenced in no less than 5 clauses in the Christadelphian Statement of Faith (the BASF).

[23] As an example of this see *"Unbelievable"*, Rob Hyndman, 2015, page 72: "The problem with reaching this conclusion is that it raises questions about the rest of scripture. Was Abraham also mythical? What about Moses, or David? If I could explain away the difficulties in Genesis by making it spiritual or "allegorical", was it acceptable to do the same with other parts of the Bible that inconveniently contradicted the observations of scientists, archeologists and historians? Was faith even falsifiable once the inconvenient parts could be allegorized?"

Not a new idea

At this point it is worth observing that the suggestion that Adam and Eve were not real historical people is not new. Christadelphians have had cause to rebut this erroneous view in years gone by. The following is a quotation from the writings of Alfred Norris, in 1964:

"In setting out his teaching on the permanence of marriage, the Lord answers his critics in terms of Genesis 1 and 2 *(Matthew 19:1-8 etc)*. God made them in the beginning male and female *(Genesis 1)*, and said, "Therefore shall a man leave his father and mother and cleave unto his wife" *(Genesis 2)*. Both the "creation records" are included in one statement, and made the basis of the true teaching on marriage. It is impossible to drive a wedge between the teaching and the history on which it is based. If such an Adam and Eve had not existed, and such a divine blessing had not been pronounced, then such a conclusion as to the sanctity of the marriage state could not validly have been drawn. Jesus must be right in his estimate of the history, or he is unreliable in his estimate of the morals"[24].

In conclusion, it is worth repeating the simple fact that *the suggestion that Adam was not a real historical person is not taught in the Bible.*

---

[24] "Where Science and Religion Meet - (1) What does the plain man do?" Alfred Norris, *The Christadelphian* 1964, Vol 101, p 436-439

9. The origin of death

"Wherefore, as by one man sin entered into the world, and death by sin; and so death passed upon all men, for that all have sinned" *(Romans 5:12)*

Death by sin

Some theistic evolutionists believe that Adam really did exist, but that he came into existence through evolution. He was the first of the human-like creatures to whom God chose to reveal Himself. If this is true, then obviously he must have been a dying creature, even before he disobeyed the commandment of God. This is a big problem for the theistic evolutionist because of the testimony of Paul in Romans 5:12: "Wherefore, as by one man sin entered into the world, *and death by sin;* and so death passed upon all men, for that all have sinned". The clear teaching of the apostle is that for man *death did not exist* prior to Adam's sin. The theistic evolutionist therefore has to maintain that Paul was not speaking about death in the *universal* sense here, because evolved humans were subject to death before Adam sinned[1]. A

---

[1] John Thomas states in Elpis Israel that Adam before the fall was *capable* of death, but not *subject to* death: "In their novitiate, Adam and his betrothed had a nature *capable* of corruption, but were not subject to death, or mortal" Elpis Israel, Part 1: *The Rudiments of the World,* chapter 2, page 73.
Adam and Eve may have been capable of death prior to the transgression, but at that stage death for them was not *inevitable.* Unlike the human race that subsequently arose from them, they were not subject to suffering, and destined to die. There was every possibility that, had they not succumbed to temptation in the garden, they would not have died. In that sense, we believe that Brother Thomas is right in saying that prior to the fall they were not mortal. In any case, according to the Biblical account, and as far as the human race is concerned, we can say with certainty that death did not exist until after Adam's transgression.

number of suggestions are made by the advocates of theistic evolution as to what "death" in Romans 5:12 means. For example:

- Paul is speaking of death here in the sense of it being the wages of sin[2]. Since the evolved humans were not under Divine law prior to Adam, although they were dying creatures like the beasts, they were not subject to death-as-the-wages-of-sin. They were unaware of Divine law and therefore not accountable to it. Therefore they are excluded from what Paul says here.

- Paul is not speaking about literal death, but *a spiritual or moral death* - something that takes man apart from God, in the sense that the access to God is now closed and can be restored only through faith[3]. Adam was excluded from the Garden because of his disobedience, and denied fellowship with God. In this sense he suffered a spiritual death.

Both of these views are *a perversion of the teaching of Paul,* and are not supported by the context of Romans 5, as we shall seek to illustrate[4].

Wherefore

The first point to note from Romans 5:12 is the very first word: *"Wherefore…".* What Paul is about to say springs out of what he has already said in 5:11: "And not only so, but we also joy in God through our Lord Jesus Christ, *by whom we have now received the atonement".* The context is that of the atonement, and what Paul is about to do is to examine the tragic sequence of events that led to man's alienation from God in the first place, and the need for that atonement which has been secured through Christ. This passage is taking the "holistic" view of the problem of sin and death, and its solution in

---

[2] "…death as a punishment for sin was introduced into the world when the first sin was committed. Prior to Adam's sin, humans lived and died as the 'beasts that perish' but as God's law was unknown, sin as a concept did not exist and therefore death as a punishment for sin simply did not apply", Ken Gilmore, *New Testament references to Adam and Eve by Paul and Jesus do not disprove evolution,* 10th November 2013. http://christadelphianevolution.blogspot.co.uk/2013/11/new-testament-references-to-adam-and.html

[3] https://biologos.org/common-questions/human-origins/death-before-the-fall

[4] For further exposition of Romans 5:12 see "Paul's Letter to the Romans", "Righteousness and Condemnation through Federal Heads", pp 60-66 (1992 edition), *John Carter,* CMPA

the atonement. Through Jesus Christ, sin can be forgiven and God and men reconciled[5]. What this means is that the doctrine of the atonement and a clear understanding of Romans 5:12 are *inextricably linked*. If we misunderstand Romans 5:12, then this will have implications for our understanding of the doctrine of the atonement. This will impact on our faith in the work of the Lord Jesus Christ, which is why Romans 5:12 must assume a focal point in our considerations of death in relation to Adam.

By one man

Paul traces the source of the problem of sin back to one man: "Wherefore as *by one man* sin entered into the world…". That man was Adam, and the circumstances of his transgression are described in detail in Genesis 3. There were far-reaching consequences of that sin, and what we need to understand is that everything that Paul says by inspiration in Romans 5:12 is traced back to that "one man", thus:

- By one man sin entered into the world
- By one man death entered into the world by sin
- By one man death passed upon all men
- By one man all sinned

This point is emphasized throughout the remaining verses of Romans 5, thus:

- "Through the offence of one many be dead"[6].
- "Judgment came by one to condemnation"[7].
- "By one man's offence death reigned"[8].
- "By the offence of one judgment came upon all men to condemnation"[9].
- "By one man's disobedience many were made sinners"[10].

---

[5] See 2 Corinthians 5:19

[6] Romans 5:15

[7] Romans 5:16

[8] Romans 5:17

[9] Romans 5:18

[10] Romans 5:19

In sharp contrast to this, *"by the righteousness of one* the free gift came upon all men to justification of life"[11]. Of course, Paul does not mean all men without exception who have ever lived will receive the free gift of life, but all men who have come into relationship with Christ by baptism into him. He is comparing Adam with Christ, and using them once again as *two federal heads.* All who are "in Adam" receive condemnation - and that is everybody - whereas all who are "in Christ" receive justification of life[12]. As the apostle says in 1 Corinthians 15, "For as in Adam all die, even so in Christ shall all be made alive"[13].

We need to be very clear in our understanding of Paul's words - sin entered into the world, and death passed upon all men, through one man. This law of death entered the world because of Adam's sin. As far as the human race is concerned death did not exist before. This is in complete harmony with Genesis 2:17, and the warning God gave to Adam that if he ate from the fruit of the tree of the knowledge of good and evil he would "surely die". This makes no sense if he was already dying before he transgressed.

The sin of Adam had consequences for the entire human race - it resulted in all of his posterity inheriting a nature that is death-stricken, and biased towards sin. But immediately after Adam and Eve fell, God Himself set in motion a chain of events whereby reconciliation would ultimately be available for sinful man, through faith in the life, death and resurrection of the Lord Jesus Christ: "Whom God hath set forth to be a propitiation *through faith in his blood,* to declare his righteousness for the remission of sins that are past, through the forbearance of God; to declare, I say, at this time his righteousness: that he might be just, and the justifier of him which believeth in Jesus"[14]. At every stage in the sacrifice of Christ the righteousness of God

---

[11] Romans 5:18

[12] This understanding of 1 Corinthians 15:22 is consistent with the teaching of other scriptures that salvation is not universal, but is dependent upon belief of the Gospel and baptism into Jesus Christ: *(Mark 16:15,16; Acts 2:38-41; John 17:3; Acts 4:10-12; Ephesians 4:4,5; Galatians 3:27-29).* Whilst all men are "in Adam", not all men are "in Christ".

[13] 1 Corinthians 15:22

[14] Romans 3:25,26

was upheld. When he, a member of the human race, and made "in the likeness of sinful flesh"[15], was put to death it was a manifest token for all to see[16] that sinful flesh merited destruction. But Jesus had not personally succumbed to the temptations of the carnal mind, and therefore he did not deserve death[17]. God's righteousness was therefore again upheld when Jesus was resurrected from the dead: "Whom God hath raised up, having loosed the pains of death: *because it was not possible that he should be holden of it*"[18]. For those who believe that the sacrifice of Jesus declared God's righteousness, God in His grace is willing not only to forgive sin, but also ultimately to remove the *source* of sin within - the carnal mind - when at the return of the Lord Jesus Christ "mortality" will be "swallowed up of life"[19].

Paul says that "by of one man... death *passed upon* all men", and the Greek word διέρχομαι - *'dierchomai'* - holds the meaning of passing through, or spreading:

- Rotherham: "And so unto all men death *passed through*".
- RSV: "And so death *spread* to all men".
- NKJV: "And thus death *spread* to all men".

If it be asked exactly how death spread to all men, the answer is self-evident - it is *by physical descent from Adam*[20]. Each subsequent generation of the human race from the time of Adam to the present has inherited from him a nature that is corruptible, prone to sin, and which leads inexorably to death.

---

[15] Romans 8:3

[16] John 3:14

[17] 1Peter 2:22, Hebrews 2:14

[18] Acts 2:24

[19] 2 Corinthians 5:4

[20] The Birmingham Amended Statement of Faith, Clause 5, puts it this way: "Adam... was adjudged unworthy of immortality, and sentenced to return to the ground from whence he was taken - a sentence which defiled and became a physical law of his being, and was transmitted to all his posterity, until the coming of Christ"

If it be objected that Paul speaks of "death", not "mortality", then we should observe that these terms are used synonymously elsewhere in the writings of Paul, for example 1 Corinthians 15:54: "So when this *corruptible* shall have put on incorruption, and this *mortal* shall have put on immortality, then shall be brought to pass the saying that is written, *Death* is swallowed up in victory".

The viewpoint of the theistic evolutionists that Adam, and evolved humans, were dying creatures prior to Adam's sin, *is not consistent with the teaching of Romans 5:12.*

What does death mean?

The theistic evolutionists cannot accept that "death" in this context relates to the inheritance of Adam's death-stricken nature by his descendants, because they postulate the evolution of human peoples before Adam, who obviously had to be mortal[21]. Death therefore has to be defined in some other way. As observed above, some theistic evolutionists propose that Paul is speaking of some sort of moral or spiritual death that is experienced now as a result of alienation from God[22]. Others suggest that "death" in Romans 5 has to be defined as "death-as-the-wages-of-sin", and it is reasoned that since the evolved humans were without law they were not under this law of sin and death, and it can therefore be maintained that Romans 5:12 is not talking about them, since they did not die as a consequence of transgression.

The problem with this view is highlighted by what Paul says next: "For until the law[23] sin was in the world: but sin is not imputed when there is no law.

---

[21] It should be noted that this understanding is at variance with the Birmingham Amended Statement of Faith, Clause 3: "That the appearance of Jesus of Nazareth on the earth was necessitated by the position and state into which the human race had been brought by the circumstances connected with the first man - *1 Cor. 15:21-22; Rom. 5:12-19; Gen. 3:19; 2 Cor. 5:19-21*"

[22] "Theistic Evolution", Carl Drews, October 2014.
http://www.theistic-evolution.com/theisticevolution.html#Death

[23] The context indicates that the "law" here is referring to the law of Moses (see reference to Moses in v14). Thus the point being made is that, in the period after Adam but before Moses, all mankind still died even though the Law was not in force.

Nevertheless death reigned from Adam to Moses, *even over them that had not sinned after the similitude of Adam's transgression*[24]. Let us for the moment assume that a race of evolved humans did exist before Adam, who were without law, and to whom sin was therefore not imputed. What Paul is saying here is that even over people who were without law, to whom sin was not imputed, and who had not sinned after the similitude of Adam's transgression, "death reigned". If this is the case, it is clear that "death" cannot be defined as death-as-the-wages-of-sin, for the precise reason that they were without law, and transgression was not imputed. Furthermore, Paul continues to make the point that *even for people without law*, "by *one man's offence* death reigned *by one*"[25]. Death even reigned over those who had not sinned after the similitude of Adam's transgression, and it reigned "by one", because all men without exception have inherited Adam's death-stricken nature. The idea of a race of mortal humans, not descended from Adam and yet co-existing with him, is therefore excluded. To suggest otherwise would mean that Adam's so-called human peers living contemporary with him began to experience death because of Adam's sin. His punishment for some inexplicable reason spread to them. This hardly makes any logical sense.

The theistic evolutionists who claim that Adam was one of the evolved humans, have to maintain that Adam was always destined to die, even before he sinned, and that Paul in Romans 5:12 was not commenting on the entrance of death-stricken nature into the human race consequent upon the sin of Adam. As we have demonstrated though, *this is not what the scriptures teach.*

For that all have sinned

The last phrase in Romans 5:12 is frequently misunderstood: "And so death passed upon all men, for that all have sinned". If by "death" we are to understand the imposition of mortality upon the whole of the human race, which is passed on by inheritance from Adam, how does this relate to individual sins? Babies are mortal, yet they do not sin, and sometimes tragically they die. The answer to this revolves around who we understand

---

[24] Romans 5:13,14

[25] Romans 5:17

Paul to be referring to when he says that *"all* have sinned". The following translations of Romans 5:12 are helpful:

- "And so death passed unto all men, for that all sinned" *(RV)*
- "And in this way death came to all men, because all sinned" *(NIV)*
- "And thus death spread to all men, because all sinned" *(NKJV)*
- "And so unto all men death passed through, for that all had sinned" *(Rotherham)*

When Paul says that *"all* had sinned", he is referring to Adam and Eve in the garden. At the time when they sinned, they constituted the *whole of the human race*, and the sentence that God passed upon them of returning to the dust of the ground was thus in effect passed upon the entire human race which was, as it were, "in the loins" of Adam and Eve at the time. All mankind sinned and therefore all mankind would face the misfortune of the consequence of sin. In a similar sense Levi is said to have paid tithes to Melchizedek when he was still in the loins of his father Abraham[26] [27]. For this reason, "death spread to all men". This makes logical sense, but the logic is totally destroyed if a race of mortal hominids, unrelated to Adam, is assumed.

Once again, the teaching of Paul through inspiration is quite clear - death passed upon all men as a direct consequence of the sin of Adam and Eve. *In*

---

[26] Hebrews 7:9,10

[27] John Thomas has the following to say on Romans 5:12: "The tribe of Levi paid tithes to Melchizedec many years before Levi was born. The apostle says, 'Levi, who received tithes, paid tithes in Abraham'. Upon the same federal principle, all mankind ate of the forbidden fruit, being in the loins of Adam when he transgressed. This is the only way men can by any possibility be guilty of the original sin. Because they sinned in Adam, therefore they return to the dust from which Adam came, 'in whom all sinned'" *Elpis Israel,* pp 128,129. This interpretation we believe was based on an unsustainable translation of Romans 5:12, as C C Walker's footnote in Elpis Israel explains. The interpretation we are advancing here is different - we are not suggesting that the whole human race sinned in Adam, otherwise consistency would dictate that because Abraham believed God all his descendants should likewise be automatically implicated in his belief, which is clearly not the case. Our argument is simply that, when Adam and Eve were placed under the sentence of death, they literally constituted the entire human race. On that basis, the entire human race was sentenced to death, and this sentence has passed to all men by physical descent. The fact that, with the exception of Jesus Christ, everyone who has lived to maturity has sinned serves only to illustrate the justice of the sentence.

stark contrast to the teaching of the theistic evolutionists, death did not exist in the human race prior to Adam's sin. Connecting this to the previous chapter, we can again clearly see that Adam was a real character, and that Genesis records actual historical events.

The creation of Adam

The creation of Adam is described in Genesis 2:7: "And the LORD God formed man out of the dust of the ground, and breathed into his nostrils the breath of life; and man became a living soul". He was a living creature, formed from the union of a body made from the ground and the breath of life. As with everything else that God made, he was declared "very good"[28]. Genesis 2 continues to describe how God made Himself known to Adam, and gave him a law. The consequence of disobedience to this law would be death, and a return to the ground from whence he was made: "And the LORD God commanded the man, saying, Of every tree of the garden thou mayest freely eat: but of the tree of the knowledge of good and evil, thou shalt not eat of it: for in the day that thou eatest thereof thou shalt surely die"[29]. Adam was given explicit warning that, should he disobey the Divine commandment, this sentence of death would be imposed *"in the day* that thou eatest thereof"*.

From this we can draw a number of conclusions:
*   Because Adam chose to disobey, the death sentence was imposed upon him. It was now inevitable that Adam would die. The same phraseology is used of the sentence of death imposed on Shimei by Solomon for disobeying the commandment to remain in Jerusalem: "And the king sent and called for Shimei, and said unto him, Did I not make thee to swear by the LORD, and protested unto thee, saying, Know for a certain, *on the day* thou goest out, and walkest abroad any whither, *that thou shalt surely die?* and thou saidst unto me, The word that I have heard

---

[28] Genesis 1:31

[29] Genesis 2:16,17

is good"[30]. Shimei had previously been given this law, and once he broke the commandment and left Jerusalem, his death was inevitable.

- Although the death sentence was imposed upon Adam, he continued to live to the age of nine hundred and thirty years[31]. The punishment for disobedience was thus not intended in his case to be *instantaneous* death, but the institution of *a process of dying*. In short, if Adam disobeyed and partook of the fruit of the tree it would become absolutely inevitable that *in process of time* he would die and return to the dust. This inevitability of death was not present within Adam before he sinned because "by one man sin entered into the world, *and death by sin*"[32].

- Adam was told that this sentence would be imposed *"in the day* that thou eatest thereof"*. Prior to his transgression, he was not under that sentence of death.

- If Adam was already destined to die, then this threat of the imposition of a return to the dust for disobedience would be meaningless.

- The apostle Paul says that "since *by man came death*, by man came also the resurrection of the dead". Death came "by man". But if Adam was a dying creature from the very beginning, together with the hominids, then death did *not* come by man. Death came by God, since the hominids - and Adam - were born with the inevitability that they would one day die. If this is true then man had no input into this process at all - it was merely his misfortune.

The record indicates that when Adam and Eve sinned, they were *subjected to a change*. When they sinned "the eyes of them both were opened, and they knew that they were naked"[33]. Before they ate of the tree, "they were both naked, the man and his wife, and were not ashamed"[34]. Having disobeyed the Divine commandment, they developed within themselves an acute

---

[30] 1 Kings 2:42

[31] Genesis 5:5

[32] Romans 5:12

[33] Genesis 3:7

[34] Genesis 2:25

awareness of good and evil, which they did not have before, and a propensity to sin, which all of Adam and Eve's posterity have similarly inherited. They knew both "good" and "evil" by experience. Paul speaks of "the law of sin which is in my members"[35], and if this law of sin had been within Adam prior to the Fall, it is hardly consistent with the testimony of the Preacher that "God made man upright"[36]. This is not a fitting description of a man with a propensity to sin. God's view of the matter is stated in Genesis 3:22: "Behold the man *is become* as one of us, to know good and evil...".

Having hearkened to the words of the serpent, and partaken of the forbidden fruit, it was now absolutely inevitable that Adam and Eve would die and return to the dust of the ground: "In the sweat of thy face shalt thou eat bread, *till thou return unto the ground;* for out of it wast thou taken: for dust thou art, and unto dust shalt thou return"[37]. Eve was also subjected to a real change after she transgressed, because God said to her, "I will greatly multiply thy sorrow and thy conception; in sorrow thou shalt bring forth children; and thy desire shall be to thy husband, and he shall rule over thee"[38]. There was also physical change within the realm of nature itself. For Adam's sake, the ground was cursed, such that he would have to toil in the sweat of his face to survive: "And unto Adam he said, Because thou hast hearkened unto the voice of thy wife, and hast eaten of the tree, of which I commanded thee, saying, Thou shalt not eat of it: *cursed is the ground for thy sake;* in sorrow shalt thou eat of it all the days of thy life; thorns also and thistles shall it bring forth to thee; and thou shalt eat the herb of the field"[39].

Paul, by inspiration, reflects on this change within God's creation on account of Adam's sin, in Romans 8: "For the creation was subjected to *vanity*, not of

---

[35] Romans 7:23

[36] Ecclesiastes 7:29

[37] Genesis 3:19

[38] Genesis 3:16

[39] Genesis 3:17,18

its own will, but by reason of him who subjected it, in hope"[40]. Clearly this did not obtain right at the beginning - the creation was not subjected to vanity before Adam and Eve fell. There was a change to "the bondage of corruption"[41], albeit "in hope", through the promise of a Saviour.

In summary we can say that the theistic evolutionary viewpoint that Adam was a dying creature before he sinned *is not scripture teaching.*

The teaching of 1 Corinthians 15

It is sometimes claimed that the teaching of Paul in 1 Corinthians 15 implies that when Adam was first created he was mortal: "And so it is written, *The first man Adam was made a living soul;* the last Adam was made a quickening spirit. Howbeit that was not first which is spiritual, but that which is natural; and afterward that which is spiritual. *The first man is of the earth, earthy:* the second man is the Lord from heaven. As is the earthy, such are they also that are earthy: and as is the heavenly, such are they also that are heavenly. And as we have borne the image of the earthy, we shall also bear the image of the heavenly"[42]. It is argued that when Adam was "made a living soul", Paul confirms that he was "of the earth, earthy", and therefore by implication mortal, before he had sinned.

We do not dispute the fact that when Adam was created out of the dust of the ground, he was indeed "of the earth, earthy", but for the reasons outlined in the footnote on page 88, we do not concede that Adam prior to his transgression could be considered to be mortal, for death was not inevitable for Adam like it is for us. He may have been *capable* of death, but at that stage in his probation death was *not a certainty;* indeed there was every possibility that, should he not succumb to temptation, he would not die at all. Adam and Eve were in a unique situation, being created "very good", and there certainly was no inevitability that they would return to the dust of the ground from whence they had been created.

---

[40] Romans 8:20

[41] Romans 8:21

[42] 1 Corinthians 15:45-49

In contrast, Jesus Christ, "the last Adam", has been made a "quickening spirit" - a life imparting spirit. Through his great victory, and in God's mercy, those who have faith in him will be granted eternal life when he comes again. Adam was created from the dust of the ground, and during his probation he lived with the possibility of death, should he fail to obey the Divine commandment given to him in the garden - and this was a sentence that would be passed on to his posterity. But Jesus Christ came into the world to impart *eternal life* to others through his victory over the flesh.

We submit therefore that the teaching of Paul in 1 Corinthians 15 does not indicate that Adam was subject to death before he sinned. His mortality was a direct product of his disobedience to the law of God, in keeping with the simple teaching of Romans 5:12: "Wherefore, as by one man sin entered into the world, and death by sin; *and so death passed upon all men, for that all have sinned*".

10. The creation of Adam and Eve

"And the LORD God formed man of the dust of the ground, and breathed into his nostrils the breath of life; and man became a living soul" (Genesis 2:7)

Are Genesis 1:26,27 and Genesis 2:7 two separate creation events?

Some theistic evolutionists put forward the view that the creation of man in Genesis 1:26-30 does not relate to the creation of Adam at all. They say that this is the development of the evolved human race by evolutionary means: "And God said, Let us make man in our image, after our likeness: and let them have dominion over the fish of the sea, and over the fowl of the air, and over the cattle, and over all the earth, and over every creeping thing that creepeth upon the earth. So God created man in his own image, in the image of God created he him; male and female created he them"[1]. The creation of Adam, according to them, is dealt with separately in Genesis 2:7: "And the LORD God formed man of the dust of the ground, and breathed into his nostrils the breath of life; and man became a living soul". In support of this erroneous view, attention is drawn to a number of supposed irreconcilable differences between Genesis 1 and Genesis 2. The two accounts are considered to be so different that they cannot possibly relate to the same historical events - and in any case, Genesis 1 is not intended to be read historically, as a true record of what God did.

---

[1] Genesis 1:26,27

This view will be rebutted in chapters 11 and 12 of this book, but here we wish to focus our attention on the specific creation of man. Is Genesis 1:26,27 referring to the creation Adam and Eve, or not?

The first point we wish to make, which is of paramount importance, is this. The assertion that Genesis 1:26,27 relates to the gradual evolution of a human-like species *has no Biblical support whatsoever.* There is no room for a gradual process of evolution, taking place over millions of years, within Genesis 1:26,27, and to suggest this is to argue from silence. Instead, "God said, Let us make man in our image, after our likeness... So God created man in his own image, in the image of God created he him; male and female created he them". The work of creation is masterfully summarised by the Psalmist, thus: "For he spake, and it was done"[2]. This is absolutely inconsistent with evolution as a mechanism of creation, and there is not the slightest hint that Genesis 1:26,27 came about by gradual change over millions of years.

Let us just suppose that Genesis 1:26,27 does speak of the evolution of humans, and that Genesis 2:7 relates to the formation of Adam as a special creation, as some theistic evolutionists suggest, and that Adam and the evolved humans were contemporary with one another. It seems very peculiar that, according to Genesis 2:5, prior to the creation of Adam, the record states that "the LORD God had not caused it to rain upon the earth, *and there was not a man to till the ground"*. Equally incongruous is the fact that Adam, having named the creatures, was not able to find "an help meet" for himself[3]. The theistic evolutionists conjecture that Cain obtained his wife from the evolved humans - and yet Adam himself was apparently unable to do the same.

Jesus' use of the Genesis account

The next point to make is that, on the authority of the Lord Jesus Christ himself, we can say with *absolute certainty* that Genesis 1:26,27 relates to the creation of Adam and Eve. In his discussion with the Pharisees on the matter

---

[2] Psalm 33:9

[3] Genesis 2:20

108

of marriage and divorce, Jesus makes a composite quotation from Genesis 1:1,1:27 and 2:24, in relation to the union of Adam and Eve as one flesh: "And he answered and said unto them, Have ye not read, that he which made them at the beginning made them male and female, and said, For this cause shall a man leave father and mother, and shall cleave to his wife: and they twain shall be one flesh"[4]. From these words of the Master we can deduce the following:

- "He which made them at the beginning" is a quotation from Genesis 1:1: "In the beginning God created the heaven and the earth".
- "Male and female" quotes Genesis 1:27: "Male and female created he them".
- "For this cause shall a man leave father and mother" is quoted from Genesis 2:24, which refers to *the union of Adam and Eve* as one flesh in marriage.
- Adam and Eve were created "in the beginning". This is hardly the case if many millions of years elapsed between Genesis 1:1 and Genesis 1:27.
- The Divine law of marriage existed from the beginning. In fact Jesus says as much in Matthew 19:8: "He saith unto them, Moses because of the hardness of your hearts suffered you to put away your wives: *but from the beginning it was not so*". To which "beginning" does this refer, if not to that of Genesis 1:1? In the book of Genesis the Hebrew ראשׁית - *'reshiyth'* - is only found elsewhere in Genesis 10:10, relating to the beginning of the kingdom of Nimrod, and Genesis 49:3, concerning Reuben as the firstborn of Jacob. There is no other "beginning" to which Jesus could be referring.
- The fact that God made Adam and Eve "one flesh" in the beginning becomes the very basis upon which men and women unite together in marriage. This law has existed "from the beginning", and this makes little sense when applied to a species of creatures, evolving over millions of years, who were ignorant of God and His laws.
- The Divine law of marriage was instituted to foreshadow the union of Christ and the ecclesia, as indicated by the apostle Paul's use of Genesis 2:24: "For this cause shall a man leave his father and mother, and shall be joined unto his wife, and they two shall be one flesh. This is a great

---

[4] Matthew 19:4,5

mystery: but I speak concerning Christ and the church"[5]. This pattern has been established "from the beginning", but again it is difficult to see how a race, evolving over millions of years, and ignorant of the laws of God, could in any way be seen as foreshadowing the exalted relationship between Christ and his bride.

The beliefs of the theistic evolutionists that Genesis 1:26 does not relate to the creation of Adam and Eve *contradicts the clear teaching of the Lord Jesus Christ.*

The use of Genesis 1:26-30 in Psalm 8
The supposition of theistic evolutionists is that the creation of man in Genesis 1:26,27 does not relate to Adam and Eve, but to the evolution of a human-like species. It is further postulated that these creatures were without law, and died like the beasts, outside of the law of sin and death. God had not revealed Himself to them, they had no knowledge of His laws, and were therefore not responsible to Him.

We would point out at this stage that all of this is pure supposition, *and is not taught anywhere in the Bible.* It is based solely on the false premise that the theories postulated in scientific circles regarding the origins of life are true.

In Genesis 1:28 God gave to man whom he had created dominion over the rest of God's creation: "And God blessed them, and God said unto them, Be fruitful, and multiply, and replenish the earth, and subdue it: *and have dominion over the fish of the sea, and over the fowl of the air, and over every living thing that moveth upon the earth*". This is a critical point to observe, because this very fact is developed in the rest of scripture, in particular by the Psalmist in Psalm 8: "What is man, *that thou art mindful of him?* and the son of man, *that thou visitest him?* For thou hast made him a little lower than the angels, and hast crowned him with glory and honour. Thou madest him *to have dominion* over the works of thy hands; thou hast put all things under his feet"[6]. God was "mindful" of man - indeed, He "visited him" - hardly a description of a race of ignorant, lawless creatures. Furthermore the Psalmist

[5] Ephesians 5:31,32

[6] Psalm 8:4-6

explains that man was created with *purpose* in mind - that of having dominion over the whole of God's creation. And ultimately this Psalm is prophetic of the final destiny of man in having dominion over "the world to come", and of being brought "to glory"[7]. Indeed ultimately the Psalm, using Genesis 1:28 as its basis, speaks of the glorification of the Lord Jesus Christ himself: "But we see Jesus, who was made a little lower than the angels for the suffering of death, crowned with glory and honour; that he by the grace of God should taste death for every man"[8].

Psalm 8 is one of *the* foundation Old Testament scriptures. Indeed it is one of the most quoted Psalms in the New Testament[9] [10]. It speaks of God's ultimate intention to put the world to come in subjection under the feet of men who have become sons of God, sanctified by the Lord Jesus Christ, and who "he is not ashamed to call... brethren"[11]. It is entirely inconsistent with this ultimate purpose of God that Genesis 1:28, the foundation text for Psalm 8, should relate to an entire race of evolved creatures who were totally ignorant of God's purpose, under no responsibility to Him, and "like the beasts that perish". Even more so, when we appreciate that in the fullest sense Psalm 8 speaks of the Lord Jesus Christ himself, whom God raised from the dead, "And set him at his own right hand in the heavenly places, far above all principality, and power, and might, and dominion, and every name that is named, not only in this world, but also in that which is to come: and hath put all things under his feet"[12]. What possible reason could there be for associating the Lord Jesus Christ with a race of lawless, ignorant evolved creatures? The genealogy of Jesus Christ very clearly traces his human

---

[7] Hebrews 2:5-10

[8] Hebrews 2:9

[9] See for example Matthew 21:16; Hebrews 2:5-8; 1 Corinthians 15:27; Ephesians 1:22

[10] For an analysis of Psalm 8, in particular its use in the New Testament, see "The Crowning of the Son of Man", *J Luke*, Psalms Vol 1, pp 137-146, CSSS. Also "The Praises of Israel", *D Fifield*, Vol 1, pp 41-49, CMPA

[11] Hebrews 2:11

[12] Ephesians 1:20-22

origins back to Adam[13]. The challenge for the theistic evolutionists who believe that humankind evolved over millions of years before Adam is to prove from scripture that the genealogy of Jesus has input from an evolved human-like race. *There is no such Biblical proof.*

After our likeness

Genesis 1:26 needs to be noted with care: "And God said, Let us make man in our image, after our likeness". Man was created after the *image* and *likeness* of God. It is instructive to consider what "image" and "likeness" means in this passage.

"Likeness" is the Hebrew רמות - *'demuwth'*, and denotes a similitude. The word occurs 25 times in the Old Testament, and clearly means a *physical resemblance*, as can be seen from the following examples:

- "Also he made a molten sea of ten cubits from brim to brim, round in compass, and five cubits the height thereof; and a line of thirty cubits did compass it round about. And under it was *the similitude* of oxen, which did compass it round about: ten in a cubit, compassing the sea round about. Two rows of oxen were cast, when it was cast"[14].
- "Also out of the midst thereof came the *likeness* of four living creatures. And this was their appearance; they had *the likeness* of a man"[15].
- "And, behold, one like *the similitude* of the sons of men touched my lips: then I opened my mouth, and spake, and said unto him that stood before me, O my lord, by the vision my sorrows are turned upon me, and I have retained no strength"[16].

We can conclude from this that when God made man in His own likeness, there was a *physical resemblance* between man and the Elohim. We have ample scriptural testimony to the truth of this:

---

[13] Luke 3:38

[14] 2 Chronicles 4:2,3

[15] Ezekiel 1:5

[16] Daniel 10:16

- "Be not forgetful to entertain strangers: for thereby some have entertained angels unawares"[17].
- "And while they looked stedfastly toward heaven as he went up, behold, *two men* stood by them in white apparel"[18].
- "And the LORD appeared unto him in the plains of Mamre: and he sat in the tent door in the heat of the day; and he lift up his eyes and looked, and, lo, *three men* stood by him: and when he saw them, he ran to meet them from the tent door, and bowed himself toward the ground"[19].

Angels were mistaken for men on numerous occasions in scripture. The question is, if Genesis 1:26,27 relates to the gradual evolution of the human race, at what point in the millions of years of evolution did this physical resemblance begin? It hardly seems appropriate to consider ape-like beings to be in the likeness of the *Elohim*. The onus lies with the theistic evolutionists to prove that angelic beings were mistaken on occasions for evolving creatures. *This cannot be proven because the Biblical support for the existence of evolving humans is lacking.*

In Genesis 5:1,2, the work of God in the creation of man in His likeness is summarised, thus: "This is the book of the generations of Adam. In the day that God created man, *in the likeness of God* made he him; *male and female created he them;* and blessed them, and called their name Adam, in the day when they were created". The careful reader will have no difficulty in picking up the verbal links with Genesis 1:26,27. Not only so, but we are also told that God "blessed them", which picks up Genesis 1:28: "And *God blessed them,* and God said unto them, be fruitful, and multiply, and replenish the earth, and subdue it". The theistic evolutionist may well be quick to point out that although it says that God "called their name Adam", it is really simply the word for man. Whilst this is true, it is also true that in *the very next verse* the record tells us that "Adam lived an hundred and thirty years, and begat a son in his own

---

[17] Hebrews 13:2

[18] Acts 1:10

[19] Genesis 18:1,2

likeness, after his image, and called his name Seth"[20]. The Spirit is clearly associating the creation of man in the image and likeness of God with Adam himself, not an evolved race. And just as God made Adam in His own likeness, and in His image, so now Adam also begat a son, in his own likeness, after his image. The connection in thought between Genesis 1:26 and Genesis 5:1-3 leaves us in no doubt that the creation of man in the image and likeness of God relates to Adam himself.

This likeness with the Elohim is shared by the rest of mankind, descended from Adam, as James illustrates in his epistle: "...the tongue can no man tame; it is an unruly evil, full of deadly poison. Therewith bless we God, even the Father; and therewith curse we men, which are made *after the similitude of God*"[21].

Let us make man in our image

In what sense was man made in the "image" of God? The explanation is to be found in 1 Corinthians 11: "For a man indeed ought not to cover his head, forasmuch as he is *the image and glory of God:* but the woman is the glory of the man. For the man is not of the woman; but the woman of the man. Neither was the man created for the woman; but the woman for the man"[22]. Man was made in "the image and glory of God", and we know from such scriptures as Exodus 33:18 and 34:6,7 that the glory of God corresponds to *His moral attributes:* "And (Moses) said, I beseech thee, shew me thy glory... And the LORD passed by before him, and proclaimed, The LORD, The LORD God, merciful and gracious, longsuffering, and abundant in goodness and truth, keeping mercy for thousands, forgiving iniquity and transgression and sin, and that will by no means clear the guilty; visiting the iniquity of the fathers upon the children, and upon the children's children, unto the third and to the fourth generation". God's glory is *His character,* hence concerning the Lord Jesus Christ, the Son of God, John said that "we beheld *his glory,* the

---

[20] Genesis 5:3

[21] James 3:8,9

[22] 1 Corinthians 11:7-9

glory as of the only begotten of the Father, *full of grace and truth*[23]. From this we can conclude that Genesis 1:26 is telling us that man was created with the capacity and the opportunity to manifest in some measure the moral characteristics of God. Here again is a significant challenge for the theistic evolutionist. How can this be true of a race of beings, supposed to have evolved over millions of years, who had no knowledge of the laws of God, and therefore no opportunity to develop the moral attributes of God revealed in His word? We need to note carefully that, even *before* man was created, God said, "Let us make man in our image". The theistic evolutionist thus has to face the anomaly that, in spite of this Divine pronouncement, for millions of years a race was evolving that had *no opportunity whatsoever* to reflect the glory of God.

The context of 1 Corinthians 11 associates the allusion to Genesis 1:26 *with the creation of Adam and Eve:* "For a man indeed ought not to cover his head, forasmuch as he is the image and glory of God: but the woman is the glory of the man. *For the man is not of the woman; but the woman of the man.* Neither was the man created for the woman; but the woman for the man"[24]. Paul is referring to the creation of Eve out of Adam's side, and the Genesis account explains that she was called woman because she was "taken *out of man*"[25]. This is a significant problem for those theistic evolutionists who believe that Genesis 1:26 refers not to Adam and Eve, who were a special creation, but to the evolution of a human-like race. The theistic evolutionists need to explain why Paul uses Genesis 1:26 in the specific context of Adam and Eve, or alternatively provide Biblical evidence for the creation of evolved woman out of evolved man in the same way that Eve was created out of Adam. *There is no such Biblical evidence.*

The creation of man in God's image is a theme that is developed in a number of places in the New Testament. The epistle to the Colossians is rooted in language that is taken from Genesis 1, and in particular in chapter

---

[23] John 1:14

[24] 1 Corinthians 11:7-9

[25] Genesis 2:23

3 the apostle exhorts his readers to "put off the old man with his deeds; and… put on the new man, which is renewed in knowledge *after the image of him* that created him"[26]. This is clearly Genesis language, and we are being invited to draw a parallel with Adam, created in the image of God. The significant thing is that the development of the new man *has its basis in knowledge of God.* It is "renewed in *knowledge".* Paul continues to describe the various spiritual attributes of the new man that have to be put on: "Put on therefore, as the elect of God, holy and beloved, bowels of mercies, kindness, humbleness of mind, meekness, longsuffering; forbearing one another, and forgiving one another, if any man have a quarrel against any: even as Christ forgave you, so also do ye. And above all these things put on charity, which is the bond of perfectness"[27]. We will have no difficulty discerning that these characteristics of the new man find their practical outworking in the life of the Lord Jesus Christ, who himself was "the brightness of (God's) glory, and the express image of his person"[28]. He is the new man that disciples of his must learn to put on. These characteristics have to be *learned,* and they have their basis in *knowledge* of the life and teaching of Jesus Christ.

What this means is that to be in the image of God begins in the mind, with an understanding of the character of God Himself. Once again, it is self-evident that this process cannot even begin in a population of lawless, ignorant creatures that know not God.

---

[26] Colossians 3:9,10

[27] Colossians 3:12-14

[28] Hebrews 1:3

Word	Meaning	Supporting passages
Image	Capacity to reflect God's moral attributes (His glory or character)	1 Cor 11:7-9; John 1:14; Col 3:9-14; Heb 1:3
Likeness	Physical resemblance	2 Chron 4:2,3; Ezek 1:5; Dan 10:16; Heb 13:2, James 3:8-9

Conclusion

In conclusion, we submit that the beliefs of the theistic evolutionists are entirely without Biblical support:

- The suggestion that Adam was not a real historical person is not taught in the Bible.
- The proposal that there was a race of dying human-like creatures, or that Adam himself was subject to death before he sinned, is not consistent with the teaching of Paul in Romans 5:12 and 1 Corinthians 15:22.
- Genesis 1:26,27 and Genesis 2:7 are not two separate creation stories. They both relate to the creation of Adam.
- The assertion that Genesis 1:26,27 relates to the gradual evolution of a human species has no Biblical foundation.
- There is no Biblical proof that the genealogy of Jesus had input from an evolved race.
- There is no evidence that evolving woman was created out of evolving man, because there is no Biblical evidence for their existence.

The speculative ideas of the theistic evolutionists simply do not stand up to scrutiny when examined in detail from a Biblical viewpoint. In their attempt to harmonise evolutionary ideas with the scriptural record they have not only undermined the doctrine of inspiration but in so doing have also removed and eroded the foundations of other essential doctrines such as the atonement and the nature of man. It is important to recognise the inherent threat that this evolutionary thinking poses to the integrity of the scriptures as a whole, and the saving truth that they contain. The words of Proverbs 22:28 come to mind: "Remove not the ancient landmark, which thy fathers have set".

11. Are Genesis 1 and 2 two different creation stories?
Part 1: Two complementary accounts

"These are the generations of the heavens and of the earth when they were created, in the day that the LORD God made the earth and the heavens" (Genesis 2:4)

Introduction

Most theistic evolutionists allege that the two creation accounts recorded in Genesis 1 and 2 are irreconcilably different. They claim that the two chapters reflect different authors, different time periods, themes and accounts of creation, as though two completely different texts had simply been compiled together and placed side by side. It is further suggested that the narratives contradict each other in several key areas. This reasoning is taken as the basis for the belief that *neither account* should be taken as literal or historical, rather that they should be viewed as stories with a teaching purpose - more like a parable - as opposed to a historical narrative that gives details of real events that took place.

The table overleaf summarises a number of ideas that have been presented in regard to this concept, in an attempt to demonstrate that Genesis 1 and Genesis 2 are significantly different:[1]

---

[1] *Israel's Two Creation Stories* (3 parts), Pete Enns, http://biologos.org

Difference	Genesis 1	Genesis 2
Literary style	Poetic	Narrative
The time it took	Six day creation	Single day creation
Order of creation	Plants were created on the day 3 and man was made on day 6, Male and female created together	Plants and herbs seem not to appear until after the creation of man. Man created then woman in two distinctive acts
Depiction of God	Transcendent, creating from a distance	A participant in the affairs of man
Method of creating	Speech	Forms, breathes and plants
Name of God	Elohim, translated "God"	Yahweh Elohim, translated "LORD God"
Man's creation	In the image of God	From the dust of the ground

For those who hold such views, the idea that Genesis contains two independent, and supposedly contradictory, accounts of creation is not really problematic because the purpose of the Genesis account is not history, but allegory. But for those who hold to the traditional view that Genesis is indeed a historical account of creation, the suggestion that Genesis 1 and 2 contradict each other is potentially serious, because it affects how we view the word of God as a whole, and it strikes at the very heart of the doctrine of the inspiration of scripture.

The purpose of the next two chapters is to examine the text of Genesis 1 and 2, and to establish that they are *not* completely different creation stories. They are not contradictory, but *two complementary parts of the same historical account* of the creative work of God. There are no grounds for dismissing the belief in the teaching of scripture that "in six days the LORD made heaven and earth, the sea, and all that in them is, and rested the seventh day"[2].

Are they really different accounts?

At the outset we would say that it is simply an assumption to regard Genesis 1 as a separate, completely different account to Genesis 2. There may be differences in specific detail and structure, but it is not necessary to conclude that therefore these are different, contradictory, non-historical events.

A parallel can be drawn with the synoptic gospel accounts of the ministry of the Lord Jesus Christ. On many occasions the gospel writers describe the same events in the Lord Jesus Christ's ministry in different ways, using different language, and sometimes highlighting different details. For example, the accounts of the healing of the centurion's servant in Luke 7:1-10 and Matthew 8:5-8 reveal certain differences in the details of the same incident. Luke says that the centurion sent friends to speak with the Lord before he came to the house[3], but in Matthew it reads as though the centurion himself was there, speaking to the Lord personally[4]. The two texts could be viewed as contradictory, but in fact they are easily reconciled, when it is recalled that servants often spoke in the name of their masters. The contradiction is thus only *apparent*, not real. It would certainly be an unjustified assumption to conclude, on the basis of such supposed textual differences, that the healing of the centurion's servant did not occur at all, and that this was simply a story with a teaching purpose. To suggest such would be to be guilty of a grave misunderstanding of the text.

The same is true with Genesis 1 and 2. Just as the separate accounts of the same events in the gospels can be harmonised, so can Genesis 1 and 2. Genesis 1 represents the "big picture", so to speak, focusing on the creation of everything we see around us, in the heavens and in the earth; whereas Genesis 2 says nothing about the creation of the earth, heavens or cosmos,

---

2 Exodus 20:11

3 Luke 7:6

4 Matthew 8:8,9

and chooses to focus upon things directly relating to *the creation of man, and his placement in the garden of Eden*. Chapter 1 is the holistic view whilst chapter 2 concentrates on the first circumstances of man. When read in this way the accounts are not contradictory at all.

"For this cause…"

Before looking in detail at Genesis 1 and 2, let it be noted that the Lord Jesus Christ himself clearly accepted these two chapters as being complementary, historical accounts of *the same creative work of God*. When challenged by the Pharisees on the subject of divorce, the Lord responded by saying: "Have ye not read, that *he which made them at the beginning* made them male and female, *and said,* For this cause shall a man leave father and mother, and shall cleave to his wife: and they twain shall be one flesh?"[5] . The Master here constructs a three-part compound quotation, in which he pieces together aspects of Genesis 1 and 2 into one narrative, as the table below demonstrates:

Matthew 19	Genesis 1 and 2
Matthew 19:4 "at the beginning"	Genesis 1:1 "In the beginning…"
Matthew 19:4 "male and female"	Genesis 1:27 "in the image of God created he him; male and female created he them."
Matthew 19:5 "And said, For this cause shall a man leave father and mother, and shall cleave to his wife: and they twain shall be one flesh?"	Genesis 2:24 "Therefore shall a man leave his father and his mother, and shall cleave unto his wife: and they shall be one flesh."

The Lord quotes Genesis 1:1,27 and 2:24 as *a composite quotation*, and by doing so he establishes the fact that "at the beginning" God made both male and female, and intended that through marriage they should become "one flesh". The Master did not regard Genesis 1 and 2 as separate, contradictory "stories". He clearly believed that the events recorded were real, and this is a vital point. The Lord is teaching us that the very principles of marriage stem from a real historical event. *"For this cause"* - because of this real historical

---

[5] Matthew 19:4-5

event of the creation of man and woman - the institution of marriage exists. It is impossible to separate the *moral teaching* of Jesus on the sanctity of marriage from the *history* on which it is based. The two either stand or fall together.

On the authority of the Lord Jesus Christ, then, we have a very sound, biblical reason to view Genesis 1 and 2 as two complementary accounts of the same historical event. The Lord believed these chapters should sit side by side as one narrative and so should we[6].

"For the man is not of the woman..."

A further Biblical proof that Genesis 1 and 2 should be considered to relate to the same creative event is found in 1 Corinthians: "For a man indeed ought not to cover his head, forasmuch as he is the *image and glory* of God: but the woman is the glory of the man. For the man is not of the woman; but the woman of the man. Neither was the man created for the woman; *but the woman for the man*"[7]. In this scripture the apostle Paul, guided by the Spirit, utilises references from both Genesis 1 and Genesis 2 to substantiate his argument that men are made in the image and glory of God, and therefore ought not to cover their heads. This is demonstrated in the table overleaf:

---

[6] For more information on this see "Jesus' reading of Genesis 1-2", Peter Heavyside, *Testimony*, September 2015, 353-355.

[7] 1 Corinthians 11:7-9

1 Corinthians 11	Genesis 1 and 2
1 Corinthians 11:7: "man… he is the image and glory of God"	Genesis 1:26: "And God said, Let us make man in our image, after our likeness…" Genesis 1:27: "in the image of God created he him; male and female created he them."
1 Corinthians 11:8: "For the man is not of the woman; but the woman of the man. Neither was the man created for the woman; but the woman for the man"	Genesis 2:20: "…for Adam there was not found an help meet for him." Genesis 2:22-23: "And the rib, which the LORD God had taken from man, made he a woman, and brought her unto the man. And Adam said, This is now bone of my bones, and flesh of my flesh: she shall be called Woman, because she was taken out of Man."

These quotations illustrate the apostolic understanding of Genesis 1 and 2, that they are part of the *same account* and should be read together. The apostle Paul elsewhere declares, "I think also that I have the Spirit of God"[8]. All his writings were the product of Divine inspiration, and are equal in authority as Scripture to the book of Genesis[9]. It is right that we should expect consistency in the teaching of scripture from Genesis all the way through to the end of the New Testament, since the true Author, the God of the Bible, is a "God of truth"[10], and He "cannot lie"[11].

In the next chapter we shall see that the so-called irreconcilable differences between Genesis 1 and 2 are not irreconcilable at all.

---

[8] 1 Corinthians 7:40

[9] See 2 Peter 1:21; 2 Timothy 3:16; 2 Peter 3:15,16; Galatians 3:8; James 2:23

[10] Deuteronomy 32:4

[11] Titus 1:2

12. Are Genesis 1 and 2 two different creation stories?
Part 2: The so-called irreconcilable differences

"Where wast thou when I laid the foundations of the earth? declare, if thou hast understanding" (Job 38:4)

Introduction

Theistic evolutionists claim that Genesis 1 and 2 cannot represent factual, historical accounts of creation, because they contain obvious differences, which are irreconcilable. From this it is argued that they are not intended to be read as historical documents. This is a very serious claim to make against the word of God, and it does not stand up to careful scrutiny. In this chapter we will review each of the so-called irreconcilable differences in the light of the New Testament commentaries on Genesis 1 and 2 that place them together as one story.

1) Literary Style

It is suggested that there are differences in *literary style* between Genesis 1 and Genesis 2 and that this indicates that the two accounts are different. We do not dispute the fact that there are indeed differences in style. Genesis 1 clearly reads as a sequential series of events, each creative day being clearly defined by the reference to "the evening and the morning" *(Genesis 1:5,8,13,19,23,31)*. There is more structure to the text than in Genesis 2.

Some scholars suggest that Genesis 1 is poetically structured[1], although others dispute this[2], on the basis that the Hebrew lacks the requisite poetic markers. It is certainly true that the creation is spoken of in poetic terms in other parts of scripture:

- "Bless the LORD, O my soul. O LORD my God, thou art very great; thou art clothed with honour and majesty. Who coverest thyself with light as with a garment: who stretchest out the heavens like a curtain"[3].

- "Where wast thou when I laid the foundations of the earth? declare, if thou hast understanding. Who hath laid the measures thereof, if thou knowest? or who hath stretched the line upon it? Whereupon are the foundations thereof fastened? or who laid the corner stone thereof?"[4]

- "Who hath measured the waters in the hollow of his hand, and meted out heaven with the span, and comprehended the dust of the earth in a measure, and weighed the mountains in scales, and the hills in a balance?"[5]

All of these scriptures are clearly poetic in form, and use poetic structure, symbol and simile. None such literary devices are found in Genesis 1, and this suggests that Genesis 1 is not in fact poetry but history. The *poetic style* in

---

[1] "The first thing to notice is that Genesis 1 is a poem. As evangelicals, we affirm that the Bible is the authoritative word of God. Therefore, we believe that the Bible is totally accurate. But that doesn't mean that we take it all literally" David Swaim, https://biologos.org/blogs/archive/maker-of-heaven-and-earth-part-3

[2] "We may at this point take issue with the claim commonly raised in our day that Genesis, as to its contents, as well as other older Biblical books falls in the category of poetry rather than history... We are utterly out of sympathy with such an attitude; for it does not conform to the facts of the case. Nothing in the book warrants such an approach. It is rather a straightforward, strictly historical account, rising, indeed, to heights of poetic beauty of expression in the Creation account, in the Flood story, in the record of Abraham's sacrifice of Isaac, in Judah's plea before Joseph, and the like. But the writer uses no more of figurative language than any gifted historian might, who merely adorns a strictly literal account with the ordinary run of current figures of speech, grammatical and rhetorical" *Exposition of Genesis*, H C Leupold, Introduction, pages 12,13. Wartburg Press, 1942

[3] Psalm 104:1,2

[4] Job 38:4-6

[5] Isaiah 40:12

the above references is used to celebrate what was done *historically* according to Genesis 1. The truth is that, even if it is accepted that Genesis 1 is structured in poetic form, this does not prove that the text of Genesis 1 is depicting different events to those of Genesis 2, or that neither are accounts of real historical events. It does not give us liberty to dismiss Genesis 1 and 2 as historical narrative. There are numerous examples of Biblical poetry which nevertheless relate to real historical events. For example:

- **The book of Lamentations** is a set of poetic laments over the destruction of Jerusalem at the hands of the Babylonians - but it would be unjustified to conclude that the details contained in them had no historical validity.
- **Exodus 15** records the song of Moses and is clearly poetic - but this does not warrant the dismissal of its content as a depiction of the historical and miraculous escape of the Israelites from the armies of the Egyptians.
- **Psalm 78** is an outline of Israel's history from the Exodus to the anointing of David. It is poetic but it is nevertheless a record of real historical events.

2) How long did it take God?

"These are the generations of the heavens and of the earth when they were created, *in the day* that the LORD God made the earth and the heavens…"[6]. This verse is used to support the notion that the "second" creation story of Genesis 2 is about a single day of creation as opposed to the six day creation in Genesis chapter 1. But this idea has to be read into the text, and is dependent upon a hyper-literal reading of Genesis 2:4. This is not in fact the idea being conveyed by the text at all. The phrase in the Hebrew is בְּיוֹם - '*byom*', and it means literally "in the day", in the sense of "when", as translated for example in the New International Version: "This is the account of the heavens and the earth when they were created. *When* the LORD God made the earth and the heavens…". The phrase does not refer to a specific 24 hour period but to a more general period of time. We use the same device in English, when we say things like "back in *the day* when we didn't have computers…".

---

[6] Genesis 2:4

Evidence of the use of the phrase in this way can be seen in other parts of the scriptures. In Numbers 7, for example, we read about the Levitical princes who made offerings on the day that the tabernacle was sanctified: "And the princes offered for dedicating of the altar *in the day* (בְּיוֹם) that it was anointed, even the princes offered their offering before the altar"[7]. The general phrase "in the day" here is not to be taken as a 24 hour period because the chapter continues to explain how the twelve princes made offerings over *twelve consecutive days*. The days are numbered for emphasis, just as they are in Genesis 1: "And he that offered his offering *the first day* was Nahshon the son of Amminadab, of the tribe of Judah... On *the second day* Nethaneel the son of Zuar, prince of Issachar, did offer..."On *the third day* Eliab the son of Helon, prince of the children of Zebulun, did offer"[8]. Each of these twelve days constituted *"the day* when (the tabernacle) was anointed", as verse 84 indicates: "This was the dedication of the altar, *in the day* (בְּיוֹם) when it was anointed, by the princes of Israel: twelve chargers of silver, twelve silver bowls, twelve spoons of gold"[9].

The same is true of Genesis 1 and 2. The individual days of creation in Genesis 1 are clearly to be understood as 24 hour periods, since they are qualified by reference to "the evening and the morning". These six days are then all incorporated into the general summary statement of Genesis 2:4: "These are the generations of the heavens and of the earth when they were created, *in the day* (בְּיוֹם) that the LORD God made the earth and the heavens"[10].

There are many other examples of similar usage elsewhere in the scriptures. For example, speaking of the restoration of the fortunes of Zion in the future Age, Micah speaks of *"the day* (בְּיוֹם) that thy walls are to be built, in that day

---

[7] Numbers 7:10

[8] Numbers 7:12,18,24. See also vv 30,36,42,48,54,60,72,78

[9] Numbers 7:84

[10] For more information on this see "Genesis 1-2 - The Duration of Creation", Peter Heavyside, *Testimony,* October 2015, 397-400.

shall the decree be far removed"[11]. This clearly does not mean that Jerusalem's walls will be rebuilt in one day, but rather "at the time when…". Similarly, the prophet Zechariah predicts the future time of Jacob's trouble at the hands of the Gentiles, and says: "Behold, *the day* of the LORD cometh, and thy spoil shall be divided in the midst of thee"[12]. We do not expect Israel's future troubles to be over in just one literal day.

3) The generations of the heavens and of the earth

The creative record of Genesis 2 begins with the phrase, "These are *the generations of* the heavens and of the earth when they were created"[13]. Other translations convey the idea of a "record", or an "account": "This is the account of the heavens and the earth when they were created" *(NIV)*. What follows in Genesis 2 is a *further account* of the creation as described in Genesis 1, when "God created the heaven and the earth"[14]. It is complementary to Genesis 1, and it supplies further details which are presented in a thematic, rather than a chronological way.

The phrase "these are the generations of…" in fact punctuates the whole of the book of Genesis, and serves to divide the book into distinct sections. The Hebrew is תולדות - '*towledot*', and it occurs a total of eleven times throughout the book[15]. It also occurs three times outside the book of Genesis[16]. Theistic evolutionists make much of the fact that the phrase begins the narrative of Genesis 2:4, and yet it is absent from the whole of the narrative of Genesis 1. This, it is suggested, confirms that Genesis 1 and Genesis 2 are two separate creation accounts. But there is no doubt that the first occurrence of the phrase in Genesis 2:4 refers back to same heavens and the earth described in the previous chapter: "These are the generations of

---

[11] Micah 7:11

[12] Zechariah 14:1

[13] Genesis 2:4

[14] Genesis 1:1

[15] Genesis 2:4; 5:1; 6:9; 10:1; 11:10; 11:27; 25:12,19; 36:1,9; 37:2

[16] Numbers 3:1; Ruth 4:18 and 1 Chronicles 1:29

the heavens and of the earth when they were created, *in the day that the LORD God made the earth and the heavens"*.

It must be observed that the phrase "these are the *generations* of the heavens and of the earth" is not intended to convey information to us about the *origin* of the universe. That this is so can be seen by comparion with the other occurrences of the "*towledot* sequence" in the book of Genesis. The *'towledot'* of Noah, for example[17], does not include details concerning his birth, but it does provide information about his life, and the subsequent birth of his sons. Likewise, the *'towledot'* of the heavens and the earth does not describe the *origin* of the universe, but what happened to the heavens and the earth *after* their creation. This helps us to understand why Genesis 1 does not begin with a "*towledot* sequence". In particular, the record emphasizes subsequent events that were to take place *on the earth*, which is why the unusual combination, "the earth and the heavens", is used[18].

4) Order of Creation

One of the cornerstone arguments[19] for suggesting that Genesis 1 is contradictory to Genesis 2 is the assertion that the order of creation in each chapter is different. Genesis 2 seems to present the creation of man before the creation of vegetation, and the formation of the beasts and the fowls appears to take place last. Genesis 1 presents the following order of things clearly labelled and set out for us:

---

[17] Genesis 6:9

[18] "The unusual combination, "earth and heaven", which only occurs in Ps. 148:13… shows that *the earth* is the scene of the history about to commence, which was of such momentous importance to the whole world" *Commentary on the Old Testament - The Pentateuch*, C F Keil & F Delitzsch, page 72

[19] "There are also strong Biblical arguments against interpreting Genesis 1 as a consecutive sequence of creation events (day or age) and that is that this results in a flat-out contradiction with the sequence of creation in Genesis 2." Ken Gilmore, The Days of Creation are not Consecutive Creation Events, Berea Portal, August 23, 2012
http://berea-portal.com/the-days-of-creation-are-not-consecutive-creation-events-1/

Day	Creation of	Genesis 1
1	Light and Dark	v2-5
2	Firmament called heaven	v6-8
3	Dry land called earth and plant life	v9-13
4	Sun moon stars	v14-19
5	Fish and birds	v20-23
6	Animal life and man	v24-31

In Genesis 2 three key subjects are covered:

Subject	Subject covered	Genesis 2
1	Watering of the earth and creation of man	v4-7
2	The garden of Eden and the placing of man within it	v8-17
3	The naming of the animals and the creation of Eve	v18-25

Genesis 1 is an account of the grand scheme of creation, whilst in Genesis 2 the account focuses in and around the key details of the creation of man himself. A few key points might be worth noting on Genesis 2 at this stage.

i) Watering of the earth and creation of man - v4-7
The Hebrew in this section is difficult to render into English, but it appears that the record is explaining the conditions that prevailed before God's creative work on earth began. The table overleaf summarises this.

Genesis 2		Meaning
v4	"These are the generations of the heavens and of the earth when they were created, in the day that the LORD God made the earth and the heavens"	This is the "account" (NIV) of what happened at "the time" when the heavens of Gen 1:6-8 and the earth of Gen 1:9-13 were created. *Note: the RV adds a full stop here indicating that what follows is a new thought.*
v5	"And every plant of the field before it was in the earth, and every herb of the field before it grew: for the LORD God had not caused it to rain upon the earth, and there was not a man to till the ground"	After days 2 and 3 the heavens had been created and so had the "dry land" of earth, but there was no life in them. This was before the plants had been created. **Also** - rain had not been instituted by God and man had not been created to till the ground.
v6	"But there went up a mist from the earth, and watered the whole face of the ground"	This describes what happened after the heavens and the earth and the plant life had been created. Moisture was provided via evaporation from the earth. This provided the sustenance for the plant life mentioned in v5.
v7	"And the LORD God formed man of the dust of the ground, and breathed into his nostrils the breath of life; and man became a living soul"	This addresses the second requirement described in v5. Man was created to "till the ground". This occurred on Day 6 according to Gen 1:26-27

At this point we are introduced to man. He has been introduced in the context of the role he was created for - to "till the ground", and to help to propagate the earth with plant life. Further detail on this is outlined in the next section.

ii) The garden of Eden and the placing of man within it - v8-17

This section defines the specific conditions of man's first surroundings and his environment. There is a description of the garden God creates in Eden. The account simply tells us that man is placed in Eden for the specific reason already outlined in verse 5 - to "till the ground", or to "dress it" - note that in the Hebrew the word translated "till" - עָבַד - '*abad*', in verse 5, is also translated "dress" in verse 15. Verses 16-17 contain the command of God to not eat of the tree of life. All of this is further detail in addition to the creation of man on the sixth day of creation, described in Genesis 1. The details provided in Genesis 1 and 2 in this regard are easily harmonised.

The advocates of the idea that there are contradictions sometimes point out that Genesis 2:9 describes the creation of plant-life, which appears to take place *after* the creation of man in Genesis 2:7. This is the reverse of Genesis 1, where vegetation is created on day 3, and man is not created until day 6. The solution to this is to read Genesis 2:9 in its context, and to appreciate that this is clearly a description of the specific plant-life *in the garden of Eden*, not plant life as a whole: "And the LORD God planted a garden eastward in Eden… and out of the ground made the LORD God to grow every tree that is pleasant to the sight, and good for food"[20]. That this is the case becomes clear from the second part of verse 9, which gives us the key information regarding the two special trees that were located specifically in the garden of Eden: "The tree of life also *in the midst of the garden*, and the tree of knowledge of good and evil".

iii) The naming of the animals and the creation of Eve - v18-25

This next section provides us with further information regarding man's responsibilities and situation. The Lord God declares in v18 that "it is not good that the man should be alone". The beasts and the fowls are brought before Adam to see what he would call them, but there was no help found for him. Because of this Eve was created from Adam's rib, and this is described in verses 21-22.

In this section the critics give two main reasons for doubting the literality of the record:

• It seems the animals are created *after* Adam contrary to Genesis 1:24-25 where they are created *before* him: "And out of the ground the

---

[20] Genesis 2:8,9

LORD God formed every beast of the field, and every fowl of the air; and brought them unto Adam to see what he would call them"[21]. The solution to this is to note that it is just as valid linguistically to render Genesis 2:19 with the pluperfect "had formed", referring to what God had already done, *prior to the formation of Adam* from the dust of the ground. Rotherham renders this verse: "Now Yahweh God *had formed* from the ground every living thing of the field, and every bird of the heavens, which he brought in unto the man, that he might see what he should call it". The NIV is similar: "Now the LORD God *had formed* out of the ground all the beasts of the field and all the birds of the air. He brought them to the man to see what he would name them".

- Adam is asked to name the animals before the creation of Eve who is created after all the beasts have come before Adam, and no "help meet" was discovered. The sceptic points out that naming all the animals in one day would have been an impossible task for Adam, and therefore the record should not be taken as literal historical fact. But this is to fail to perceive the main point that is being established in Genesis 2:19,20, namely that of all the cattle, the beasts of the field, and the fowl of the air, *Adam was unable to find a help meet for himself.* This is where the emphasis lies, not on the supposition that Adam was called upon to give names to every single creature that God had made. It would have been sufficient for Adam to encounter all the creatures dwelling in the garden or some select representative animals that God determined to bring to him to demonstrate to him that

---

[21] Genesis 2:19

there was no companion with whom he could enjoy fellowship[22] [23]. It is also noteworthy that in any case the record only mentions the "cattle", the "fowl of the air" and the "beasts of the field". There is no mention of "creeping things" or "fish of the sea"[24].

The chapter concludes with a description of the creation of Eve as a help meet for Adam. As we have pointed out, this can be read in perfect harmony with the events of Day six in Genesis 1.

5) Different depictions of God & method of creation

The theistic evolutionists suggest that Genesis 1 gives a *transcendent* description of God but in Genesis 2 we have a more *anthropomorphic* depiction (human characteristics applied to God), and that this is good evidence for Genesis 1 and 2 representing two differing stories.

Advocates of this view assert that the description of God's method of creating is evidence for this. In Genesis 1 God *speaks*, and it is done. In Genesis 2 God *forms, breathes and plants*, which, it is suggested, are all human based concepts. But this is a very poor argument, and careful reading reveals

---

[22] "The time when this took place must have been the sixth day, on which, according to chap. i. 27, the man and woman were created: and there is no difficulty in this, since it would not have required much time to bring the animals to Adam to see what he would call them, as the animals of paradise are all we have to think of". Genesis, *Commentary on the Old Testament,* C F Keil & F Delitzsch, Vol. 1, Page 87.

[23] "Is it necessary to assume that the angels led to Adam all the enormous variety of creatures already made? A wide and diverse selection, those living in the garden, would surely suffice to demonstrate to Adam's high intelligence (no Neanderthal low-brow!) that amidst them all he was really alone (apart from his occasional fellowship with the angels). The animals learned that Adam was their master, made to have dominion (Ps 8:6), and in turn he was impressed with their essential inferiority. Thus, one of Adam's first school subjects (though not *the* first) was zoology". *Genesis 1-4,* Harry Whittaker, Page 71.

[24] Genesis 1:24,26

that God's activity is also described in anthropomorphic terms in chapter 1, where He "called," "saw," and "rested"[25] [26].

6) Different names of God used

In Genesis 1 God is described as *'Elohim'*, whereas in chapter 2 He is *'Yahweh Elohim'*. This is put forward as a further indication that the two accounts should be viewed as being different, perhaps with different authors. But this is mere assumption and the argument is unconvincing. In scripture differences in the Divine name and titles are placed in the text for *a purpose*:

- **Elohim**, meaning "mighty ones"[27] conveys the idea of *strength*. The concept of the angels completing the work of God is certainly incorporated within Genesis 1:26: "And God said, *Let us make man* in *our* image, after *our* likeness".
- **Yahweh**, meaning "He who will be"[28] is often connected in scripture to God's glory and purpose revealed in others.

It is not justified to assume that the use of *'Elohim'* in Genesis 1, and *'Yahweh Elohim'* in Genesis 2, indicates that the chapters have different authors, or tell different stories. As we are dealing with the word of God then we must conclude that God may have chosen a different style deliberately, for a purpose. Genesis 1 is a description of the whole of God's creative work, and so it is reasonable that the might of God's creative power should be emphasized. Genesis 2 focuses on the creation of man, the pinnacle of God's creation, and the only creature capable of displaying and manifesting God's glory. It is therefore appropriate that in Genesis 2 the memorial name of Yahweh should be used.

---

[25] Genesis 1:8,12; 2:2,3

[26] "It should… be borne in mind that chapter one…offers certain very prominent anthropomorphisms, which may very well be classed as arguing a conception of God no different from that of the next two chapters. A trifling difference, which may not even be worthy to be called a difference of style, is exaggerated to the point of being made to appear as a radical difference" *Exposition of Genesis,* H C Leupold, page 107, Wartburg Press, 1942

[27] "The Memorial Name", *Phanerosis*, John Thomas, Page 65 (Logos edition)

[28] "Ehyeh And Yahweh", *Phanerosis*, John Thomas, Page 137 (Logos edition)

7) The creation of man

It is claimed by the theistic evolutionists that Genesis 1 and 2 give two different stories, and contain contradictory statements, regarding the creation of man. Genesis 1:27 says that "God created man in his own image, in the image of God created he him; male and female created he them", whereas Genesis 2:7 states that "the LORD God formed man of the dust of the ground, and breathed into his nostrils the breath of life; and man became a living soul". Whilst it is true that there is a difference in the description of the way man is created, there is no contradiction. Genesis 1 informs us that man was made in the image of God, whereas Genesis 2 gives us specific details of *how* man was created.

Conclusion

The assertion that Genesis 1 and 2 are two different accounts is flawed, and has to be read into the text[29]. On the authority of the Lord Jesus Christ's use of Genesis 1 and 2 in Matthew 19, and on the apostle Paul's use in 1 Corinthians 11, we must see Genesis 1 and 2 as the *same account*, speaking of the *same events at the same time period*. They are historical and literal accounts, and we can and must believe and trust them. We have a choice - to believe in God's inspired word, or to seek to undermine this by trusting in the ideas and

---

[29] It ought to be noted that the controversy regarding whether or not Genesis 1 and 2 contain two different creation accounts is not new. In 1861, John William Burgon MA, fellow of Oriel College, Oxford, gave a series of seven lectures at the University of Oxford, in response to a volume entitled "Essays and Reviews", in which many of the ideas currently being promoted by theistic evolutionists were put forward. One of the contributors to "Essays and Reviews" was C W Goodwin MA. In his preliminary remarks, Burgon has this to say: "After what is evidently intended to be a showy sketch of the past history of our planet, - "we pass" (says Mr Goodwin) "to the account of the Creation contained in the Hebrew record. And it must be observed that in reality two distinct accounts are given us in the book of Genesis; one, being comprised in the first chapter and the first three verses of the second; the other, commencing at the fourth verse of the second chapter and continuing till the end. This is so philologically certain that it were useless to ignore it" (p 217). Really we read such statements with a kind of astonishment which almost swallows up sorrow. Do they arise, (to quote Mr Goodwin's own language,) "from our modern habits of thought, and from the modesty of assertion which the spirit of true science has taught us?" (p 252) Convinced that my unsupported denial would have no more weight than Mr Goodwin's ought to have, I have referred the dictum just quoted to the highest Hebrew authority available, *and have been assured that it is utterly without foundation" Inspiration and Interpretation*, Preliminary Remarks, xcii, J W Burgon MA

opinions of man: "Trust in the LORD with all thine heart; and lean not unto thine own understanding"[30].

---

[30] Proverbs 3:5

13. Is Genesis 1 a vision?

"And God saw every thing that he had made, and, behold, it was very good. And the evening and the morning were the sixth day" (Genesis 1:31)

In an attempt to open up the possibility of an evolutionary approach to creation some theistic evolutionists adopt the idea that the numbered days in Genesis 1 are not days in which God created the "heavens and the earth", but instead represent days in which God revealed the detail of His creation to an author by means of a series of visions. The author then subsequently wrote down what he saw on the day that each vision was given. This is often referred to as the "Days of Revelation Theory", the "Revelatory-day Theory" or the "Vision Theory"[1] [2].

The purpose of this chapter is to review this idea from a scriptural perspective, and to illustrate that it holds no credibility if an honest and unbiassed reading of the text is maintained.

---

[1] One of the original propagators of the vision theory idea was PJ Wiseman who published a book entitled *"Creation Revealed in Six Days"* (Marshall, Morgan, and Scott, Ltd., 1948). See http://www.angelfire.com/mo/launchingpad/index.html See also The Seven Days of Revelation Theory, Steven L. Ross, http://graceandknowledge.faithweb.com/slross.html

[2] The idea was proposed within the Christadelphian community by Ralph Lovelock and Alfred Norris, Jr. See *"A Prologue to Revelation"*, The Christadelphian 1940, Volume 77, Pages 106-108. It should be noted that Alfred Norris used this idea, not in favour of theistic evolution but in an attempt to seek to accommodate long geological ages.

Historical Narration

The main problem with the vision theory is that there is no obvious or clear textual indication that we are to understand the Genesis 1 account as anything other than a literal account of creation that actually occurred over six days. The language of Genesis 1 is that of historical narrative, where consecutive days are listed, and the events that took place in each day recorded[3]. The language is not that of dramatic vision as is found, for example, in the prophets or in the book of Revelation. The following are examples of dramatic visionary narrative:

- *"I beheld* the earth, and, lo, it was without form"[4].
- "After this *I saw* in the night visions, and behold a fourth beast, dreadful and terrible"[5].
- "And *I John saw these things,* and heard them. And when I had heard and seen, I fell down to worship before the feet of the angel which shewed me these things"[6].

In each case the text tells us very clearly that the inspired writers saw something, a vision, which they could see with their eyes and hear with their ears. This is not the language of Genesis 1. In Genesis 1 it is not a prophet that "sees" - rather it is *God Himself.* For example: "And *God saw* the light"[7], *"God saw* that it was good"[8]. We therefore conclude that in Genesis the text is not reporting visionary appearances but literal facts.

Since there is no clear textual indication that Genesis 1 is a vision, it seems unlikely that this viewpoint would have ever been proposed had there not been a perceived necessity to harmonise the text of Genesis with the theories of modern science. The idea that Genesis 1 is an account of a vision given to

---

[3] Numbers 7 is another good example of this textual structure.

[4] Jeremiah 4:23

[5] Daniel 7:7

[6] Revelation 22:8

[7] Genesis 1:4

[8] Genesis 1:10

the inspired writer, and not the actual creation itself, is an unjustified assumption that is not supported by the text of scripture.

"For in six days"

Not only is there no clear indication in the text that Genesis 1 is a vision, but other accounts of creation found elsewhere in scripture provide no support for the idea either. Rather they demand that the six creative days be understood literally. Consider these verses from Exodus:

- "But the seventh day is the sabbath of the LORD thy God: in it thou shalt not do any work, thou, nor thy son, nor thy daughter, thy manservant, nor thy maidservant, nor thy cattle, nor thy stranger that is within thy gates: *For in six days the LORD made heaven and earth, the sea, and all that in them is*, and rested the seventh day: wherefore the LORD blessed the sabbath day, and hallowed it"[9].

- "Wherefore the children of Israel shall keep the sabbath, to observe the sabbath throughout their generations, for a perpetual covenant. It is a sign between me and the children of Israel for ever: *for in six days the LORD made heaven and earth*, and on the seventh day he rested, and was refreshed"[10].

The phrase "heaven and earth" in these references from Exodus links directly to the exact words in the header statement of Genesis 1:1: "In the beginning God created the *heaven and the earth*". This intertextual link ties these phrases to Genesis 1 and helps us understand the Genesis 1 account. On the authority of these statements from Exodus alone, we can conclude with certainty that the six days of Genesis 1 are indeed to be understood literally. It has been suggested that Exodus 20:11 was inserted into the text[11] by a scribe some time after Exodus was written, but there is no evidence for

---

[9] Exodus 20:10,11

[10] Exodus 31:16,17

[11] "Exodus 20:1-17 clearly stands out from its immediate context in Exodus 19:9-25; 20:18-21, as in Exodus 20:1 God speaks directly whereas in the context, with its central theme of theophany, Moses is mediator of God's words... All this suggests that Exodus 20:1-17 has been secondarily inserted into its present context." *Methods for Exodus,* Thomas B Dozeman, page 123

this. Moreover, even if this were true, we would have no justification for disregarding it as not part of inspired scripture. In any case, the very same wording occurs in Exodus 31:17, and this verse cannot be explained away as a scribal insertion.

"The Lord made heaven and earth"

The word for "made" in Exodus 20:11 and 31:17 is the Hebrew *'asah'* (עָשָׂה). It is used in other parts of scripture in the context of creation, thus:

- "And God saw every thing that he had *made*, (עָשָׂה) and, behold, it was very good"[12].
- "O come, let us worship and bow down: let us kneel before the LORD our *maker* (עָשָׂה)"[13].
- "For all the gods of the nations are idols: but the LORD *made* (עָשָׂה) the heavens"[14].
- "O LORD, how manifold are thy works! in wisdom hast thou *made* (עָשָׂה) them all: the earth is full of thy riches"[15].

Advocates of the visionary theory[16] point out that the verb *'asah'* can also mean "to do", as is apparent from within Exodus 20 itself: "Six days shalt thou labour, and *do* all thy work: but the seventh day is the sabbath of the LORD thy God: in it thou shalt not *do* any work, thou, nor thy son, nor thy daughter, thy manservant, nor thy maidservant, nor thy cattle, nor thy stranger that is within thy gates: for in six days the LORD *made* heaven and earth, the sea, and all that in them is, and rested the seventh day: wherefore

---

[12] Genesis 1:31

[13] Psalm 95:6

[14] Psalm 96:5

[15] Psalm 104:24

[16] "Read in the sense of its use in other passages in the same documents, the word 'asah' would not convey to them the meaning of creation in six days, but of something done in six days." P J Wiseman, *"Creation Revealed in Six Days"*, Chapter 3 - Current Theories and the Fourth Commandment, (Marshall, Morgan, and Scott, Ltd., 1948).

the LORD blessed the sabbath day, and hallowed it"[17]. They also emphasize that the word is used in passages where the context is clearly that of revelation. For example:

- "And Moses said unto the people, Fear ye not, stand still, and see the salvation of the LORD, which he will *shew* (עָשָׂה) to you to day…"[18].
- "And he said unto him, If now I have found grace in thy sight, then *shew* (עָשָׂה) me a sign that thou talkest with me"[19].
- "*Shew* (עָשָׂה) me a token for good…"[20].
- "Wilt thou *shew* (עָשָׂה) wonders to the dead? shall the dead arise and praise thee? Selah"[21].

Clearly '*asah*' cannot be constrained simply to the idea of making or creating. It also has the meaning of *doing something*[22], and exactly what is being done has to be determined by the context. In the case of the above references, it is the revelation itself that is being "done". In the case of the occurrences in the sabbath law of Exodus 20 what is being done is general work.

"In the beginning God created"

Genesis 1:1 states that "in the beginning God *created* the heaven and the earth". Significantly, a different Hebrew word - '*bara*' (בָּרָא) - is used here, and '*bara*' has a number of meanings including "to form, fashion by cutting,

---

[17] Exodus 20:9-11

[18] Exodus 14:13

[19] Judges 6:17

[20] Psalm 86:17

[21] Psalm 88:10

[22] Heb. עָשָׂה - *Asah:* "Do, perform, make something, perform a work, act with effect, produce, yield, bring about". *The Brown-Driver-Briggs Hebrew and English Lexicon*, Francis Brown DD D.Litt., Hendrickson Publishers, 1996.

shape out, make, or create"[23]. This is in keeping with the fact that what is taking place in Genesis is not the revelation of a vision but rather the *actual creation* of the things described in the remainder of the account.

It is legitimate to ask why in Exodus 20 the word *'asah'* meaning "to do or make" is used, instead of the word used in Genesis 1:1, *'bara'*, "to shape out or create". The words do carry similarities of meaning, but there must be a reason why God, through inspiration, chose two different words. The context of Exodus 20 is that of the Sabbath law, and it has been suggested that the work of God in creation is being compared with the everyday work that man does for six days of the week. Whilst a man might not be *creating* things each day, he will be engaged in *doing work*. Therefore, to ensure the sabbath law is understood clearly the word "do" is used instead of the word "create". A comparison is being drawn between what *God* did in Genesis 1 (i.e. create the heavens and the earth) and the general work being done by *man* during the days of the working week.

Irrespective of the reason for this difference in words between Exodus and Genesis, we submit that there is nevertheless no justification for the suggestion that what God had "done" over the six days of Genesis 1 was to reveal His creative work in a series of visions. This is an assumption that has to be read into the text. In contrast, the inspired account of Genesis 1:1 tells us very clearly what it is that God did - He created "the heaven and the earth". We submit that a simple reading of Genesis 1 leads us to the conclusion that it was *the work of creation itself* that was accomplished in six days.

If we were expected to understand Genesis 1 as a series of night visions, then we would expect Exodus 20 to say something like, "For in six days Yahweh *revealed in vision* the creation of the heavens and the earth and on the seventh day ceased to reveal". But this is not what the text says. Instead, we are given

---

[23] Heb. ברא - *Bara:* "Shape, create, form, fashion by cutting, shape out, pare a reed for writing, a stick for an arrow". *The Brown-Driver-Briggs Hebrew and English Lexicon,* Francis Brown DD D.Litt., Hendrickson Publishers, 1996. In the Authorised Version, *'bara'* is translated as follows: create (42x), creator (3x), choose (2x), make (2x), cut down (2x), dispatch (1x), done (1x), make fat (1x).

a simple Divine commentary on Genesis 1, and both are in complete harmony. There is no room here for any other understanding, than that the work of creation took place over a time period of 6 literal days, and on the 7th literal day God ceased from His work. This understanding of the 6 day creation of the heaven and the earth is consistent with other scriptures where God is praised for His creative work in this regard:

- "For thus saith the LORD that created (בָּרָא) the heavens; God himself that formed the earth and made it; he hath established it, he created it not in vain, he formed it to be inhabited: I am the LORD; and there is none else"[24].

- "Thus saith God the LORD, he that created (בָּרָא) the heavens, and stretched them out; he that spread forth the earth…"[25].

- "Praise him, ye heavens of heavens, and ye waters that be above the heavens. Let them praise the name of the LORD: for he commanded, and they were created (בָּרָא)"[26].

"God ended his work which he had made"

Genesis 2:2-3 says that "on the seventh day God ended his *work* which he had made; and he rested on the seventh day from all his *work* which he had made. And God blessed the seventh day, and sanctified it: because that in it he had rested from all his *work* which God created and made". The Hebrew word מְלָאכָה - *'mĕla'kah*[27] is translated here as "work" in each case.

---

[24] Isaiah 45:18

[25] Isaiah 42:5

[26] Psalm 148:4,5

[27] Heb. מלאכה - *mĕla'kah:* "Occupation, work, labour, business, work as something done or made, workmanship". *The Brown-Driver-Briggs Hebrew and English Lexicon,* Francis Brown DD D.Litt., Hendrickson Publishers, 1996.

Some advocates of the visionary theory[28] suggest that this word is an inflection of the word 'mal'ak' which means "angel" or "messenger". This is then connected with the word "work" and the conclusion is drawn that what is being described in Genesis 2:2-3 is the work of a messenger who has revealed the vision of creation to the inspired author.

This view holds a number of unjustified assumptions. If it is correct to understand the word 'mĕla'kah' as carrying with it the idea of angelic vision then we would be justified in seeking similar usage of the word elsewhere in scripture, but we find no such usage. Instead, the scriptures use the word *consistently* to simply denote labour, or work. One such example is found in Genesis 39 in relation to the life of Joseph: "And it came to pass about this time, that Joseph went into the house to do *his business* (מלאכה - translated "work" YLT NKJ ESV NET ASV and "duties" in NIV); and there was none of the men of the house there within"[29]. Nobody would suggest that we are to read into this a reference to some sort of angelic visionary work - such a conclusion would be absurd. There is no hint of this and to propose such an idea would be to make nonsense of the text, yet this is the type of argument that is being advocated by those who see in the word 'mĕla'kah' in Genesis 2:2-3 a reference to an angelically mediated vision.

It is interesting to observe that this word also appears in the account of the Sabbath law in Exodus 20: "Six days shalt thou labour, and do all thy work (מלאכה): But the seventh day is the sabbath of the LORD thy God: in it thou shalt not do any work (מלאכה), thou, nor thy son, nor thy daughter, thy manservant, nor thy maidservant, nor thy cattle, nor thy stranger that is

---

[28] "However, *mla'ktow* is an inflection of the word *mla'ak*, which is consistently translated as "angel" throughout the Old Testament. Since we could also translate angel as ambassador, here we could translate *mla'ktow* as a deputation, a delegated task, or even an angelic revelation. We see it used in that sense in Haggai 1:13: 'Then spake Haggai the Lord's messenger in the Lord's MESSAGE unto the people,….". This supports the suggestion that Genesis 1 records six days of an angelic message about God's creation." Steven L. Ross, *"Genesis Said It First"* (second edition, 1991), *"The Seven Days of Revelation Theory"* which can be read here: http://graceandknowledge.faithweb.com/slross.html

[29] Genesis 39:11

within thy gates"[30]. Again we have a clear connection to Genesis 1 and 2. *'Mĕla'kah'* has nothing to do with angelic visions, and the meaning of the commandment is clear - the children of Israel were to cease from their labour which they had been doing, on the seventh day. The reason for them to cease from *their* labour and work is because *God had done likewise* in the beginning. Therefore God's work in Genesis 1 is compared again to the work that men do.

We submit that it is little more than wishful thinking to seek to attach a meaning of angelic visions to the Hebrew word מְלאָכָה. This word is not used in this way in scripture.

"Evening and morning"

Advocates of the visionary theory suggest that the occurrence of the phrase "evening and morning" in Genesis 1 indicates that the days were days in which a vision was given[31] [32]. A comparison is drawn between Genesis 1:5 and Daniel 8:26 which was indeed a vision:

---

[30] Exodus 20:9,10

[31] "During the daylight hours of each of the six successive days (each divided by an evening and a morning, when man rested) God revealed to him something new about creation, and during the first three days gave to man the names of the things He had revealed. When at the end of the six days God had finished talking with man He instituted the seventh day as a rest day for man's sake. In six days God had revealed "the heavens and the earth and all that in them is", and the six days occupied in this work were followed by a day of rest. As Dillmann says, "God blessed the seventh day and hallowed it, that is not later on, but just then on the seventh day." P J Wiseman, *"Creation Revealed in Six Days"*, Chapter 4: "Towards A Solution" (Marshall, Morgan, and Scott, Ltd., 1948)

[32] "Let it be suggested, then, that in Genesis 1:1–2:3, we have an account of an apocalyptic prologue to the story of the Bible, in its prime concern with the relationship of man to his Maker, presented to the visionary consciousness of the seer in seven daily visions, until the whole has passed before him, to be written by him for us.
A day, in this view, is a genuine day, but it is a day in which the work of unspecified times is presented to Moses and to us: in the visions of six days he sees and tells the story of the cardinal facts of creation, culminating, so far as its work is concerned, with the sixth day's creation of man; and reaching its divine climax in the divine rest of the seventh." Ralph Lovelock and Alfred Norris, Jr. *"A Prologue to Revelation"*, The Christadelphian 1940, Volume 77, Page 107

- **Genesis 1:5**: "And the evening (Heb. עֶרֶב - *'ereb'*) and the morning (Heb. בֹקֶר - *'boqer'*) were the first day"[33].
- **Daniel 8:26**: "And the vision of the evening (עֶרֶב - *'ereb'*) and the morning (בֹקֶר - *'boqer'*) which was told is true: wherefore shut thou up the vision; for it shall be for many days".

The meaning of these two Hebrew words can be determined by how they are used elsewhere in scripture. For example:
- **Exodus 18:13** "And it came to pass on the morrow, that Moses sat to judge the people: and the people stood by Moses from the morning (בֹקֶר) unto the evening (עֶרֶב).
- **Psalm 55:17**: "Evening, (עֶרֶב) and morning, (בֹקֶר) and at noon, will I pray, and cry aloud: and he shall hear my voice."
- **Numbers 28:8**: "And the other lamb shalt thou offer at even (עֶרֶב): as the meat offering of the morning (בֹקֶר), and as the drink offering thereof, thou shalt offer it, a sacrifice made by fire, of a sweet savour unto the LORD."

The simple teaching of these passages is that the phrase correlates to *a whole day*, marked by the rising and the setting of the sun. Throughout the scriptures this phrase is used in connection with all manner of things that are said to take place within this set period. To attempt to draw a connection with the vision of Daniel 8, and attach the meaning of a vision to Genesis 1, is an unwarranted assumption. One could just as easily draw a connection with the theme of prayer in Psalm 55. The difference between the Genesis account and Daniel 8 is that in Daniel 8 we are clearly told that this was the period of time that Daniel received his vision. This is not the case in Genesis 1. In contrast, there is no indication in the text of Genesis 1 that a series of visions is being portrayed.

The singular Day
Genesis 2:4 says: "These are the generations of the heavens and of the earth when they were created, in the day that the LORD God made the earth and the heavens". Some who hold the visionary theory propose that the use of

---

[33] See also Genesis 1:8,13,19,23,31

the singular form of the word "day" indicates that the account or record of the creation of the "heaven and the earth" was made on one singular day[34].

The meaning of the phrase "in the day" has been examined at length in the previous chapter. The phrase in the Hebrew is literally "in the day", in the sense of "when", as translated for example in the New International Version: "This is the account of the heavens and the earth *when* they were created. When the LORD God made the earth and the heavens...". The phrase does not refer to a specific 24 hour period but to *a more general period of time*.

It is unsustainable to associate the phrase "the generations of the heavens and of the earth" with a singular day of creation. The creation of the "heavens" is recorded on day 2 in Genesis 1:6-8, and the creation of the earth is recorded on day three in Genesis 1:9-13. Thus this passage in Genesis 2:4 should be seen as an overview statement and not a reference to a singular part of the creation record.

Conclusion

Having reviewed the main arguments for the visionary theory we conclude that there is no evidence to support the notion that Genesis 1 represents a series of visions. The text does not warrant this. Other references to the work of creation in the Bible do not hint at the record being that of vision, particularly Exodus 20:11 and Exodus 31:17, which state unambiguously that "in six days the LORD made even and earth". Attempts to explain the Revelatory Day Theory do so on faulty logic, making words mean things which they do not, and putting forward ideas which do not hold water in the light of the teaching of the other scriptures. It is an argument from silence to understand Genesis 1 as a series of visions.

---

[34] "Note the singular form of the word 'day' in Genesis 2:4, which seems to refer to all seven days of creation. All the other traditions suppose that God simply uses the word 'day' loosely here... However, if we view the days of Creation as seven consecutive days of revelation to Moses, then Genesis 2:4 can literally function as a statement that God revealed the story of Adam and Eve in the Garden and the Fall of Man to Moses during the same day that he gave his first evening and morning revelation about creation to Israel.
In contrast to how badly other interpretations fit the verse, this more literal approach fits this verse so well that Genesis 2:4 provides a major support for the Seven Days of Revelation view of the Creation Story." Steven L. Ross, *"Genesis Said It First"* (second edition, 1991), *"The Seven Days of Revelation Theory"*. http://graceandknowledge.faithweb.com/slross.html

It comes down to our acceptance of the authority of the scriptures of truth. If God has told us that He created the heavens and the earth in six days then it is not our prerogative to seek to interpret this differently. It is always easy to find reasons to doubt, it is less easy to believe, but this is what we are called upon to do. The principle of Romans 10 is worth considering: "So then faith cometh by hearing, and hearing by the word of God"[35].

If the word of God tells us that the creation was completed in six literal days, that "he commanded, and they were created"[36], then we must have faith in this. God cannot lie[37], and therefore we can, and must, trust in His word. We therefore maintain that the six days of creation in Genesis 1 are an account of historical facts, that "in six days the LORD made heaven and earth, the sea, and all that in them is"[38].

---

[35] Romans 10:17

[36] Psalm 148:5

[37] Titus 1:2

[38] Exodus 20:11

14. The question of Cain's wife

"And Cain went out from the presence of the LORD, and dwelt in the land of Nod, on the east of Eden. And Cain knew his wife; and she conceived, and bare Enoch: and he builded a city, and called the name of the city, after the name of his son, Enoch" (Genesis 4:16,17)

Introduction

Over the years, the issue of where Cain obtained his wife from has been used on numerous occasions by Bible sceptics, in a bid to discredit the Bible, and particularly the book of Genesis as a true historical account of how the human race began. Perhaps most well-known is the famous "Scopes monkey trial" that took place in Tennessee in 1925[1]. This was a legal case in which a high school teacher, John Scopes, was accused of violating legislation that made it unlawful to teach human evolution in any state funded school. Scopes was unsure whether he had ever actually taught evolution, but he purposely incriminated himself so that the case could have a defendant.

At the trial, William Jennings Bryan stood for the prosecution on behalf of the Christian faith. He was interrogated by the defence attorney, Clarence Darrow, on the question of Cain's wife, and Bryan was unable to answer the questions put to him. In spite of the prosecution's poor performance, Scopes was found guilty and fined $100, but the verdict was overturned on a technicality. The world press seized on this story, and it was presented as a

---

[1] https://en.wikipedia.org/wiki/Scopes_Trial

victory for the evolutionists. The Christians were said to be unable to defend the truth of the Bible, upon which their faith was based[2].

It is ironic that this very same issue which has been used to ridicule the Christian faith is now being used by those who, whilst professing the Christian faith, are seeking to accommodate evolutionary ideas into the record of the early chapters of Genesis. The argument is put forward that the wife of Cain must have been obtained from a race of humans that had arisen by process of evolution, and that lived at the same time as Adam and Eve[3].

Not a new view

It ought to be pointed out that this is not a new view in ecclesiastical history. The suggestion that a race of pre-Adamites existed was advanced by the Calvinist Isaac la Peyrère in 1655 at Bordeaux[4], although he eventually abandoned the belief, and was converted to Roman Catholicism. Even

---

[2] In 1960 a film entitled "Inherit the Wind" was produced, starring Spencer Tracy, Frederic March and Gene Kelly. This was a fictionalised account of the 1925 Scopes monkey trial, and was very critical of Biblical creationism.

[3] It is worth noting that in 1848 John Thomas put forward the view that there may have been a "pre-Adamic" creation: "There are indeed hints, casually dropped in the scriptures, which would seem to indicate that our planet was inhabited by a race of beings anterior to the formation of man" (*Elpis Israel*, chapter 2, The creation of the earth and man, page 10). But it must be stressed that Bro Thomas in no way believed that members of that creation were still in existence at the time of the creation in Genesis 1. He suggests that whatever took place on earth before the unfolding of the Genesis creation was completely destroyed: "This probably consisted in the total wreck of their abode, and their entire submergence, with all the mammoths of their estate, under the waters of an overwhelming flood. Reduced to this extremity, the earth became "without form and empty; and darkness overspread the deep waters" *(Genesis 1:1)*. Its mountains, hills, valleys, plains, seas, rivers, and fountains of waters, which gave diversity of *"form"* to the surface of our globe, all disappeared; and it became *"void"*, or empty, no living creatures, angels, quadrupeds, birds, or fishes, being found any more upon it" (*Elpis Israel*, chapter 2, The creation of the earth and man, page 11). We should observe that the beliefs of John Thomas advanced here are entirely different to those who maintain that there was a pre-Adamic race that came into existence by process of evolution, and with whom Adam and his offspring were able to intermarry. These are two very separate things. Our early brethren never accepted evolution as an explanation of creation.

[4] https://en.wikipedia.org/wiki/Isaac_La_Peyrère

within Christadelphian circles, the suggestion has arisen from time to time, almost from the beginning of the community's history.

- In 1888 Frank Shuttleworth had reason to write a couple of short articles in *The Christadelphian* magazine refuting the view that the issue of Cain's wife suggested the existence of a race of people that did not descend from Adam: "To say that Adam was not the only man then existing on the face of the earth is to introduce confusion into a matter that left alone is simplicity itself; more than that, it is to introduce an element that is entirely excluded by all the facts of the case. To ask the question, "Where did Cain get his wife from?" is of no avail against such an all-excluding account. It might just as well be asked where did Lamech get his two wives from? or, on the other side, where did Seth (the father of Enos) get his wife from (5:6), and those by whom he was immediately succeeded? The answer is before us, in such statements as the following: "Adam begat sons and daughters;" "Seth begat sons and daughters;" "Enos begat sons and daughters;" "Cainan begat sons and daughters;" "Mahalaleel begat sons and daughters;" "Jared begat sons and daughters;" "Enoch begat sons and daughters;" "Methuselah begat sons and daughters;" "Lamech begat sons and daughters." To suggest that in the first instance wives were obtained from another race, altogether outside Adam and his descendants, is to seek to account for the posterity of Cain and Seth on principles that take the bottom out of the whole record, and that give the human race a start inconsistent with the unity of the race, on which the work of Christ on behalf of both Jew and Gentile is based; and which will at last include results "out of every kindred, tongue, people, and nation" (Rev. 5:9). Paul establishes the matter beyond all controversy in his address to the Gentile Athenians (Acts 17.) in saying so expressly that "God who made the world hath made of one blood all nations of men for to dwell on all the face of the earth" and determined both "the times and bounds of their habitation""[5].

- The issue reared its head again in the wake of the controversy surrounding the publication of Ralph Lovelock's views, and in the September 1965 edition of *The Christadelphian magazine*, the editor, L.G. Sargent, made the following observation regarding the supposition

[5] F. Shuttleworth, *The Christadelphian Magazine*, Vol. 25 (1888), pp. 618-619, 679-781.

that there was a pre-Adamite race from whence Cain obtained his wife: "Why should members of a pre-Adamite race avenge a murder in Adam's family? What concern would it be of theirs? The difficulty arises from assuming that none of Adam's "sons and daughters" were born before Seth, whereas all we are justified in saying is that Seth was "appointed" in place of Abel and was designated as the ancestor of the line which brought forth Noah, Abraham and Christ. It does not prove that there were no other existing children... Fears as to the effect of evolutionary teaching are for the future as its implications come to be followed out, rather than for those who advance it in the first place. That these dangers are real is only too clearly exemplified in the churches around us, with their vapid, emasculated and humanised theology. Are we to go the same way?"[6]

The fears that L.G. Sargent gave voice to back in 1965 are now sadly proving to be well grounded. The same arguments are being put forward again within our community, with the primary objective it seems of attempting to harmonise the scriptures with evolutionary theory. In recent times there has been a shift in thought within certain sectors of our community, and instead of esteeming the scriptures of truth as being completely authoritative, now it is the scientific theories of men that are held out to be absolutely unquestionably true, and the word of God has to be brought into line with modern scientific thought. The end result of this is that brethren and sisters are beginning to question the very foundation of their faith, they are being "tossed to and fro, and carried about with every wind of doctrine, by the sleight of men"[7], and some have lost their faith altogether[8]. This is an absolute tragedy.

The purpose of this chapter is to go back to first principles, and to establish that the supposition that Cain married a female human who did not descend from Adam and Eve is *entirely without foundation*, and that there is sufficient

[6] L. G. Sargent, *The Christadelphian Magazine,* Vol 102 (1965), p. 417.

[7] Ephesians 4:14

[8] See, for example, Bro. Rob Hyndman's blog post, *"An end of faith"*: http://robjhyndman.com/musings/unbeliever/#more-2410

information given in the scripture record to make such a conclusion unnecessary.

The historicity of Adam and his family

The first point to make is that, contrary to what some theistic evolutionists believe, Adam and Eve were real historical people. In every single reference to Adam and Eve in the Bible, their historicity is taken absolutely for granted, and without question. The apostle Paul states unambiguously that "Adam was first formed, then Eve"[9]. The Genesis account establishes that Eve was "the mother of all living"[10], and to this the apostle agreed when he declared to the Athenians on Mars' hill that God "giveth to all life, and breath, and all things; and he made of one every nation of men for to dwell on all the face of the earth"[11].

Similarly, with regards to Adam and Eve's offspring, Cain and Abel, the scriptures unite with one voice to confirm that they were real historical people. Concerning Cain, the apostle John testifies that he "was of the wicked one, and slew his brother... because his own works were evil, and his brother's righteous"[12]; and concerning the ungodly who had crept into the ecclesia in his days, Jude says that "they have gone in the way of Cain"[13]. The Lord Jesus Christ himself makes the observation that Abel was "righteous"[14] - and if Abel was not a real historical figure, here was the perfect opportunity for the Jews, who were always seeking to ensnare the Lord in his words, to say so. Yet they were silent on the matter of Abel's historicity. The writer to the Hebrews observes that Abel had faith, and

---

[9] 1 Timothy 2:13

[10] Genesis 3:20

[11] Acts 17:26 RV

[12] 1 John 3:12

[13] Jude v 11

[14] Matthew 23:35

"obtained witness that he was righteous"[15]. Moreover, he states categorically that "these all died in faith"[16], and if Abel did not really exist, he did not really die in faith, and the apostle's argument is made null and void.

There can be no doubt, then, that the scriptures teach that Cain and Abel were real historical individuals, the children of Adam and Eve, and that Cain through jealousy slew his brother Abel, because "his own works were evil, and his brother's righteous".

The birth of Cain

The birth of Cain, the elder, is recorded in Genesis 4:1: "And Adam knew Eve his wife; and she conceived, and bare Cain, and said, I have gotten a man from the LORD". We are not told how old Adam and Eve were when Cain was born. Seth was born when Adam was 130 years old, according to Genesis 5:3, at which point Cain and Abel were clearly mature human beings, capable of keeping sheep and tilling the ground, and Cain was old enough to kill his brother. The genealogy in Genesis 5 illustrates that future generations of men in the line of Seth had their firstborn sons between the ages of 65 and 182 years. It is quite possible that Adam and Eve may have begun to have children considerably earlier than this, since they were created in the beginning as mature human beings.

The record *does not say* whether Cain was Adam and Eve's firstborn child. It is noteworthy that part of the punishment imposed upon Eve by God on account of her disobedience was that her sorrow and her conception would be increased: "Unto the woman he said, I will *greatly multiply* thy sorrow *and thy conception;* in sorrow thou shalt bring forth children; and thy desire shall be to thy husband, and he shall rule over thee"[17]. Eve's ability to conceive was thus to be increased, and it may well be therefore that Adam and Eve had other offspring before Cain was born. It is not possible to be certain either way.

---

[15] Hebrews 11:4

[16] Hebrews 11:13

[17] Genesis 3:16

Cain's murder of his brother

In process of time, Cain and Abel brought their respective offerings to God. Abel's offering was accepted, and Cain's was not, and in his jealousy Cain slew his brother: "And Cain talked with Abel his brother: and it came to pass, when they were in the field, that Cain rose up against Abel his brother, and slew him"[18]. For this murderous act, Cain was condemned by God to be "a fugitive and a vagabond... in the earth"[19].

Cain clearly found his punishment unjust, and complained to God: "And Cain said unto the LORD, My punishment is greater than I can bear. Behold, thou hast driven me out this day from the face of the earth; and from thy face shall I be hid; and I shall be a fugitive and a vagabond in the earth; and it shall come to pass, *that everyone that findeth me shall slay me*"[20]. Here is strong evidence that there existed in the earth at this time a significant number of people, *who had descended from Adam and Eve*, and who would seek to avenge the blood of Abel, their close relative. Those who believe in the existence of a pre-Adamic evolved race race put forward the idea that Cain was expressing his fear of the pre-Adamites - but as L.G. Sargent pointed out, what possible reason could a race of unrelated beings have for seeking to execute vengeance on Cain? It makes much more sense to see this as a reference to Cain's own kith and kin, who would seek to avenge the murder of Abel.

Cain departs from the presence of the LORD

Motivated by the fear of retribution, Cain went out from the presence of the LORD and dwelt in the land of Nod. After his departure, the record states that *"Cain knew his wife;* and she conceived, and bare Enoch: and he builded a city, and called the name of the city, after the name of his son, Enoch"[21]. We are not told how long it was after his departure that Cain's wife bare Enoch. Neither are we specifically informed where Cain met his wife. It is an

---

[18] Genesis 4:8

[19] Genesis 4:12

[20] Genesis 4:13,14

[21] Genesis 4:17

unnecessary assumption to conclude that Cain's wife came from the land of Nod, and therefore did not originate from his own family. Nothing in the plain reading of the text demands this understanding. It is perfectly possible that Cain may have been already married when he left Eden, and that he took his wife with him when he departed for the land of Nod.

Significantly, the record states that "Cain knew *his wife...*"[22]. The Hebrew here is אִשָּׁה - *'ishah'* - which is the name Adam gave to Eve in Genesis 2:23: "She shall be called *Woman* - אִשָּׁה - because she was *taken out of Man*". In a typical sense, what was literally true of Eve also becomes symbolically true of every other female member the human race - by marriage the woman is declared by the husband to be "bone of my bones, and flesh of my flesh". But if it is supposed that Cain's wife was not, in fact, a member of the Adamic race, then it is not true in any sense that she was "taken out of man" - she was not אִשָּׁה - rather she was a member of a race of creatures that had no relation to the Adamic line whatsoever.

The theistic evolutionists assume that there would not be enough people for Cain to be able to build a city in the land of Nod. But we note that the record *does not say* how long it took for Cain to build the city, indeed it may have taken many hundreds of years, by which time the population may have risen considerably. Owing to the fact that in the ante-diluvian world death was somewhat of a rarity, the population of the world at the end of Cain's life may have reached several million.

The birth of Seth

After the murder of Abel, the record says that "Adam knew his wife again; and she bare a son, and called his name Seth: For God, said she, hath appointed me another seed instead of Abel, whom Cain slew"[23]. It is often assumed that at this point Adam and Eve had only two children - Cain and

---

[22] ibid

[23] Genesis 4:25

Seth - and therefore Cain must have obtained his wife from elsewhere[24], but this is an unjustified conclusion. Concerning the birth of Seth, Genesis 5 says that "Adam lived an hundred and thirty years, and begat a son in his own likeness, after his image; and called his name Seth: and the days of Adam after he had begotten Seth were eight hundred years: and he begat sons and daughters: and all the days that Adam lived were nine hundred and thirty years: and he died"[25]. Seth was born when Adam was 130 years old, and in addition to Cain and Seth, Adam begat other sons and daughters. Whilst the record says that Adam "begat sons and daughters" after commenting on the birth of Seth, this does not give us liberty to conclude that the "sons and daughters" were only born *after* the birth of Seth. Note that in the genealogy of Genesis 5, for each generation subsequent to Adam, the record says that "sons and daughters" were born after the birth of the particular son highlighted in the record. Thus, for example, concerning Seth it says that "Seth lived an hundred and five years, and begat Enos: and Seth lived after he begat Enos eight hundred and seven years, *and begat sons and daughters*"[26]. It is an unjustified assumption to conclude that sons and daughters were born to Seth only *after* the birth of Enos. Genesis 5 gives nine generations, beginning with Adam, and in each case "sons and daughters" are mentioned only after the birth of the particular son mentioned in the genealogy. Are we to suppose that in *nine successive generations* daughters were only born after sons? Given that the probability of bearing a son or a daughter in any one generation is 1:2, it follows that the probability of nine successive generations having only daughters after sons is a highly improbable 1:512!

---

[24] "Cain slew Abel, and when his murder was brought to light, he expressed a fear "that *everyone* that fainted me shall slay me". This was not an imaginary fear. God expressed its danger by giving Cain a sign that everyone finding him should not slay him. Thus it is quite clear that there existed contemporaries willing to avenge murder. It will not do to say he feared his unborn brothers or sisters. The fact that Seth was given to fill Abel's place and Eve received him as such shows there were no other existing sons to do so. Further, Cain went out from the Presence of the Lord and married a wife before Adam had daughters". Ron Storer, *The Christadelphian Magazine,* Vol 102 (1965), pp. 416,417.

[25] Genesis 5:3-5

[26] Genesis 5:6,7

What this means is that the phrase, "and he begat sons and daughters", is a general statement, indicating that *throughout the life of the individual concerned*, many sons and daughters were born. It does not indicate that "sons and daughters" were born only after the particular son highlighted in the genealogy. It is therefore quite possible that Adam and Eve had daughters before Seth, perhaps even before Cain and Abel. They may even have had other sons that we are not told about. In fact, as already mentioned, nowhere in the record does it state specifically that Cain was Adam's *firstborn* son - he may have been, but the record is silent on this matter.

The testimony of Josephus

Whilst not authoritative, the following quotation from the writings of Josephus is nevertheless interesting: "Adam and Eve had two sons. The elder of them was named Cain, which name, when it is interpreted, signifies a possession; the younger was Abel, which signifies sorrow. *They had also daughters…* Now, Adam, who was the first man, and made out of the earth (for our discourse must now be about him), after Abel was slain, and Cain fled away on account of his murder, was solicitous for posterity, and had a vehement desire for children, he being two hundred and thirty years old; after which time he lived other seven hundred, and then died. *He had indeed many other children*, but Seth in particular. As for the rest, it would be tedious to name them; I will therefore only endeavour to give an account of those that proceeded from Seth"[27].

Cain's wife descended from Adam and Eve

In summary, we submit that there is *no Biblical evidence* for the suggestion put forward by theistic evolutionists that Cain married an evolved female human. The scriptures do not identify Cain's wife, but the testimony of Acts 17 indicates that she must have descended from Adam and Eve: "God… *made of one* every nation of men for to dwell on all the face of the earth"[28]. All men have been made "of one" - and this flatly contradicts the supposition that the human race that exists today may have had input from a race of pre-Adamic hominids. Similarly, Paul in Romans 5 testifies that *"by one man* sin entered

---

[27] Josephus, *Antiquities of the Jews,* Chapter 2, sections 1 and 3.

[28] Acts 17:24-27

into the world, *and death by sin*[29]. Clearly Cain's wife died, and Paul says that death entered into the world because of the sin of one man. The idea of a pre-Adamic race contradicts the simple teaching of the apostle.

We conclude, therefore, that Cain married a female member of Adam's family - either his sister, or another female relative[30].

Objections from the Law of Moses

This suggestion usually provokes an objection from the advocates of theistic evolution, that close family relationships are forbidden under the Law of Moses, thus:

* "The nakedness of thy sister, the daughter of thy father, or daughter of thy mother, whether she be born at home, or born abroad, even their nakedness thou shalt not uncover"[31].
* "And if a man shall take his sister, his father's daughter, or his mother's daughter, and see her nakedness, and she see his nakedness; it is a wicked thing; and they shall be cut off in the sight of their people: he hath uncovered his sister's nakedness; he shall bear his iniquity"[32].
* "Cursed be he that lieth with his sister, the daughter of his father, or the daughter of his mother. And all the people shall say, Amen"[33].

The following factors, however, must be taken into consideration:
1) The Law of Moses was not in force at the time of Adam and Eve. Therefore the early generations were not bound by the Mosaic code. The Law forbade sexual relations with half-sisters[34], and yet Abraham

---

[29] Romans 5:12

[30] Whilst not authoritative, it is interesting to note that according to The Book of Jubilees, an ancient Jewish religious text, Cain married his sister Awan. It also mentions that Seth married his sister Azura. https://en.wikipedia.org/wiki/Book_of_Jubilees#Content

[31] Leviticus 18:9

[32] Leviticus 20:17

[33] Deuteronomy 27:22

[34] Leviticus 18:11

married Sarah, of whom he said to Abimelech, "And yet indeed *she is my sister;* she is the daughter of my father, but not the daughter of my mother; and she became my wife"[35]. Abraham was never condemned for marrying Sarah. The Law forbade a man from marrying two sisters[36], and yet Jacob married Rachel and Leah, and did so blamelessly.

2) These laws were given to Israel *for a specific purpose* - to ensure that the Israelites did not adopt the sexually immoral ways of the Canaanites, whom God cast out from before them: "After the doings of the land of Egypt, wherein ye dwelt, shall ye not do: and after the doings of the land of Canaan, whither I bring you, shall ye not do: neither shall ye walk in their ordinances"[37]. "And ye shall not walk in the manners of the nations, which I cast out before you: for they committed all these things, and therefore I abhorred them"[38].

3) From the medical point of view, it is easy to understand why marriages between close relatives were prohibited. By the time the Law of Moses was instituted, genetic errors would have been introduced into the human race, and if brothers and sisters sharing the same genetic errors married, they would be more likely to pass on such mutations to their offspring[39]. By prohibiting such close liaisons, these genetic errors would be cancelled out. At the time of Adam and Eve, the genetics of the human race would have been relatively mutation-free, which was one reason why men and women had such long life-spans. It was therefore less important for marriages between close family members to be forbidden.

---

[35] Genesis 20:12

[36] Leviticus 18:18

[37] Leviticus 18:3

[38] Leviticus 20:23

[39] It is likely that this was the cause of gigantism in such people as the Nephilims *(Genesis 6:4)* and the Anakims *(Deuteronomy 2:10,11)*. Similarly, an inhabitant of Gath, probably a relative of Goliath, had a genetic disorder known as polydactyly *(2 Samuel 21:20),* which is inherited as an autosomal dominant trait.

Conclusion

In conclusion, we submit that there is *no evidence* that Cain married an evolved human, and the case of the identity of Cain's wife cannot be used to prove the existence of a pre-Adamic race. The suggestion that Cain's wife was not descended from Adam and Eve is an argument based upon supposition and uncertainty.

In contrast, the Bible teaches clearly that:
* All men are descended from Adam.
* All men die because of sin that was introduced into the world by one man.

In these last days when the truth of the Bible is being questioned, even by members within the Christadelphian community itself, we would do well to heed the sombre warning of the prophet: "To the law and to the testimony: if they speak not according to this word, it is because there is no light in them"[40].

---

[40] Isaiah 8:20

15. Conclusions

"For the time will come when they will not endure sound doctrine; but after their own lusts shall they heap to themselves teachers, having itching ears; and they shall turn away their ears from the truth, and shall be turned unto fables" (2 Timothy 4:3, 4)

Concluding statement

We believe that the teaching of theistic evolutionists should be rejected and opposed for the following reasons:

- Because it is unscriptural.
- Because it leads to a denial of the authority of the word of God.
- Because this, in turn, can lead to a lack of appreciation of the importance of observing the commandments of God, and may produce in consequence a moral decline.
- Because it places undue reliance upon the changing beliefs of scientists, and diminishes the importance of the word of God as the basis and evidence of our faith.
- Because it is not compatible with the simple teaching of scripture that sin and death entered into the world "by one man".
- Because it undermines the teaching of scripture concerning the atonement.

How theistic evolution contradicts the Birmingham Amended Statement of Faith

The authors of this book believe that a good summary of the Gospel of salvation is provided by the Birmingham Amended Statement of Faith (BASF), which serves as the basis of fellowship that exists between all brethren and sisters in the Christadelphian Central Fellowship. It may be helpful to list the clauses in the BASF that impinge on the relevant doctrines with which the teachings of theistic evolutionists are incompatible, thus:

1) The foundation Clause

"That the book currently known as the Bible, consisting of the Scriptures of Moses, the prophets, and the apostles, *is the only source of knowledge concerning God and His purposes* at present extant or available in the earth, and that the same were wholly given by inspiration of God in the writers, and are consequently without error in all parts of them, except such as may be due to errors of transcription or translation".

2) Clause 1

"That the only true God is He who was revealed to Abraham, Isaac and Jacob, by angelic visitation and vision, and to Moses at the flaming bush (unconsumed) and at Sinai, and Who manifested Himself in the Lord Jesus Christ, as the supreme self-existent Deity, the ONE FATHER, dwelling in unapproachable light, yet everywhere present by His Spirit, which is a unity with His person in heaven. *He hath, out of His own underived energy, created heaven and earth, and all that in them is*".

3) Clause 3

"That the appearance of Jesus of Nazareth on the earth was necessitated by the position and state into which the human race had been brought *by the circumstances connected with the first man*".

4) Clause 4

"*That the first man was Adam, whom God created out of the dust of the ground* as a living soul, or natural body of life, "very good" in kind and condition, and placed him under a law through which the continuance of life was contingent upon obedience".

5) Clause 5

"That Adam broke this law, and was adjudged unworthy of immortality, and sentenced to return to the ground from whence he was taken - *a sentence which defiled and became a physical law of his being, and was transmitted to all his posterity*".

6) Clause 6
"That God, in His kindness, conceived a plan of restoration which, *without setting aside His just and necessary law of sin and death,* should ultimately rescue the race from destruction, and people the earth with sinless immortals".

7) Clause 7
"That He inaugurated this plan *by making promises to Adam,* Abraham, and David, and afterwards elaborated it in greater detail through the prophets".

8) Clause 10
"That being so begotten of God, and inhabited and used by God through the indwelling of the Holy Spirit, Jesus was Emmanuel, God with us, God manifested in the flesh - yet was, during his natural life, of like nature with mortal man, being made of a woman, of the house and lineage of David, and therefore a sufferer, in the days of his flesh, *from all the effects that came by Adam's transgression, including the death that passed upon all men,* which he shared by partaking of their physical nature".

9) Clause 12
"That for delivering this message, (Jesus) was put to death by the Jews and Romans, who were, however, but instruments in the hands of God, for the doing of that which He had determined before to be done, namely, the condemnation of sin in the flesh, through the offering of the body of Jesus once for all, as a propitiation to declare the righteousness of God, as a basis for the remission of sins. All who approach God through this crucified, but risen, *representative of Adam's disobedient race,* are forgiven. Therefore, by a figure, his blood cleanseth from sin".

10) Doctrine to Be Rejected Number 1
"That the Bible is only partly the work of inspiration - *or if wholly so, contains errors which inspiration has allowed"*.

The beliefs of theistic evolutionists
In sharp contrast to the teaching of scripture outlined in the above clauses from the BASF, belief in the false notion of theistic evolution leads to the following unscriptural conclusions:

- The Bible is not the only source of knowledge concerning God and His purpose. God is the Author of two books - the book of His word, and the book of His works, by which is meant the testimony of the realm of nature as defined by modern scientific understanding. Both books are authoritative.
- Science has confirmed evolution to be unquestionably true. Therefore Genesis 1 and 2 cannot be understood to be a literal, historical account of the creation of heaven and earth, and all that is in them.
- The early scriptures were written by men who lived in the socio-historic context of ancient near eastern civilization, and they brought with them a mistaken and primitive worldview of the origin and composition of the universe. They believed in a solid-domed sky, and this belief is reflected in the Genesis account of the creation of the firmament.
- The Bible accommodates the mistaken beliefs of the ancient writers, such as a solid firmament, and the real existence of demons. Whilst scripture is "inspired" by God, it also reflects the unscientific beliefs of the writers, and therefore contains factual errors.
- Genesis 1 and 2 is a figurative representation of the formation of the world, upon which life evolved over millions of years by process of evolution.
- Genesis 1 and 2 are two separate, contradictory accounts of the origin of life upon the earth, thus highlighting that neither account is to be understood literally.
- God did not create heaven and earth, and all that is in them, in six days. The process took place over millions of years.
- The human race is mortal because man evolved that way. Man's mortality has little to do with the initial transgression of Adam.
- Adam was not the first man. There was a race of men that evolved before the time of Adam, and Adam's children intermarried with them.
- Adam may not have existed as a real historical person at all. He may have been simply an archetypal figure.
- Assuming that Adam was a real person, he may not have been created out of the dust of the ground as a living soul, but he probably evolved in Africa about 200,000 years ago. In effect, he was the first evolved human with whom God could "do business".

- Adam was a mortal, dying creature before he transgressed. His mortality was not a sentence placed upon him by virtue of his transgression - he was already mortal.
- Because Adam may not have been a real person, it follows that God cannot have made a promise with Adam.
- Death that passed upon all men does not mean the sentence of mortality. It is probably a figurative death, indicating a state of alienation from God. Alternatively, it may indicate death-as-the-wages-of-sin, and therefore has no bearing upon those human beings that are ignorant of God's law.
- Jesus was not "a representative of Adam's disobedient race" if Adam did not exist as a real person.

Concluding appeal

The reader will readily appreciate that the beliefs of theistic evolutionists are simply not compatible with the simple truth of the Gospel, that is summarised by the Birmingham Amended Statement of Faith. The writers of this book appeal to all who love the Truth to make their voices heard on its behalf. Individuals and ecclesias espousing the above erroneous ideas are becoming more widespread and increasingly tolerated. They should be resisted if we are to value the basis of salvation - the saving truth of the Gospel message[1] and the work of the Lord Jesus Christ in overcoming the consequences of Adam's sin.

---

[1] Romans 1:16

Printed in Great Britain
by Amazon

28785214R00099